THE METAVERSE AND THE FUTURE OF FASHION

Nov. 2023

Jennifer,
Thank you for your support. Really means a lot!

Love,
Sonia

THE METAVERSE AND THE FUTURE OF FASHION

HOW THE NEW INTERNET ERA WILL REVOLUTIONIZE THE FUTURE OF FASHION COMMERCE

SONIA PRETA

MANUSCRIPTS
PRESS

COPYRIGHT © 2023 SONIA PRETA
All rights reserved.

THE METAVERSE AND THE FUTURE OF FASHION
How the New Internet Era Will Revolutionize the Future of Fashion Commerce

ISBN
979-8-88926-764-5   *Paperback*
979-8-88926-765-2   *Ebook*

For Avi, who goes beyond simply holding the door and breaks down my walls.

*For Billy and Max, who teach me
something new every day.*

*For my parents, who instilled their courage
to embrace the unknown.*

CONTENTS

	INTRODUCTION	11
PART I	**THE WHY OF WEB 3.0, THE METAVERSE, AND FASHION**	**19**
CHAPTER 1	DISCOVERING THE METAVERSE	21
CHAPTER 2	ONLINE SHOPPING—WHAT HAS BEEN MISSING?	33
CHAPTER 3	SELF-EXPRESSION	43
PART II	**THE WHAT OF WEB 3.0, THE METAVERSE, AND FASHION**	**53**
CHAPTER 4	GAMING AND VIRTUAL WORLDS	55
CHAPTER 5	EXTENDED REALITIES—XR, AR, MR, VR	65
CHAPTER 6	NFTS AND THE BLOCKCHAIN	77
PART III	**A PEOPLE PERSPECTIVE**	**89**
CHAPTER 7	BENEFITS FOR CONSUMERS	91
CHAPTER 8	A CREATOR'S PARADISE	101
PART IV	**A BRAND PERSPECTIVE**	**111**
CHAPTER 9	BENEFITS FOR BUSINESS	113
CHAPTER 10	RISKS AND THE COST OF INACTION	125
CHAPTER 11	WHERE TO START	135
CHAPTER 12	CONCLUSION	145
	ACKNOWLEDGMENTS	153
	APPENDIX	159

Life is full of surprises. Always be ready for change because it's coming.

—MARIA PRETA, MY MOM

INTRODUCTION

I have always been an early adopter and a self-proclaimed futurist. Before the iPod came out, I owned every MP3 player, forgoing the popular Sony Walkmans. I used the Psion digital organizer before the smartphone was invented. And as a girl, I would sometimes wear trends before they hit the stores—I was fortunate to grow up with a dressmaker mother. I would watch runway shows on CNN and then sketch the next season's looks that she brought to life for me.

When I first ventured into the internet, it wasn't just for browsing. Nor was it to make a purchase, as that didn't exist yet, except for the index of books that was early Amazon. I had a deeply personal reason. I needed emotional support.

I was a newlywed and faced with an ectopic pregnancy that implanted in my fallopian tube and was not going where it needed to go. My doctor suggested a treatment of methotrexate, a chemotherapy drug used for cancer patients that would "kill the rapidly producing cells of the product of conception." My other option was to have surgery and possibly lose my tube.

As a total workaholic, I had no time to get a second opinion. The thought of getting chemo to end a mis-lodged pregnancy was overwhelming and scary. I wanted to speak to other women who had undergone the same treatment, but it was too uncommon, and my doctor pressed me for a decision.

So for the first time, I turned to the internet. It was January 1998. I searched the Netscape browser for the words "methotrexate + ectopic." To my surprise, I found a forum of fifteen women who had faced the same ordeal. This was a decade before Facebook groups existed, and I believed no one in the world could understand what I was going through.

These women welcomed me, and for eight long weeks, I chatted with them every night after work over the internet through messages. They helped me make my decision, and we bantered about life, but mostly, we confronted our biggest fear together: "Will we be able to bear children?" They became my rock and supported me through two chemo treatments and the surgery I eventually underwent when the chemo didn't work. Connecting with them on a human level was exactly what I needed.

This experience made me a believer in technology for good and has stayed with me throughout my career. I knew I wanted to become an expert however I could so that I could use technology in my life to get access to the right people and the right information whenever I needed it. It even influenced my decision to become an e-commerce pioneer at the retailer I started working for.

But throughout these past two decades, I've watched the evolution of the internet, and I believe something's still missing from the online experience. E-commerce sites offer convenience, but they lack inspiration and a human touch. I've often wondered, *what if there were a way for retailers and brands to bring back the connectivity and the excitement of shopping?*

Then, in 2021, I stumbled on the concept of Web 3.0 and the Metaverse. This immersive internet with virtual worlds intrigued me, and I devoured everything I could about this new frontier. I read books from Mathew Ball and Cathy Hackl, listened to countless podcasts, joined groups on WhatsApp and Telegram, and attended real-world meetups.

I decided I needed to experience it firsthand. So, for the first time, I entered a 3D internet experience—a metaverse world. I made an avatar with the pink hair I had always wanted to try and walked into an immersive virtual expanse. It was then that I realized I had entered the internet that the fashion industry was always destined for. The career journey that led me to that point, from the early days of the internet itself, came rushing back to me and made perfect sense.

In my early career at Saks Fifth Avenue, my ability to forecast trends and predict what customers wanted from our various brands allowed me to progress rapidly. I may have been influenced by a decade of *Style* with Elsa Klensch mixed with my mother's training about body types tied to preferred silhouettes. When I heard of Saks Inc.'s stealth plan to build a web store from the ground up, I jumped at the chance to be a part of it, even though my friends and colleagues were saying they would never buy clothes online. I was not going to miss this opportunity, and it was a career highlight to be there when we flipped the switch to go live with saks.com.

Sometime after the website launch, I continued on to Victoria's Secret, learning from great leaders how to master a growth strategy for a billion-dollar direct-to-consumer brand. Their method for customer personas was brilliant, and it was gratifying when the CEO integrated my own spin on it. With two toddlers at home, I eventually moved on from the company to launch my own start-up. And with some help, I built my own website for the first time.

I built my site with my team in 2008, eight years after the Saks site. At that time, there were still hundreds of fashion brands that were wary of launching e-commerce on their websites, worried that selling direct-to-consumer would compete with their retail accounts. Later, as a consultant, a large vertical retail brand with a website asked me to help them rebuild their site from scratch. They rushed it the first time, and their redesign was turning customers away.

This process of rebuilding sites to be more intuitive for the customer became a recurring theme for other brands I worked with. These past two decades for fashion brands and retailers have involved a lot of testing, learning, and adjusting. Some retailers—for example, Barney's and Lord & Taylor—showed the world that being a late adopter can be a costly mistake and someday lead to liquidation.

We've been in this web era for twenty or so years, and very little has changed with the online shopping format. Online stores are almost identical to each other, with similar navigation, lots of boxes and squares, and endless scrolling. A BigCommerce consumer spending report found that 54.5 percent of Americans still preferred shopping in person, but more than half believed the online benefits were worth the trade-off (BigCommerce 2021). Many people start their shopping journey online before they go into a store — 63 percent (Mohsin 2022). Online shopping is convenient and works well for searching, but it's not fun, so many have turned to social apps for inspiration.

In the 2010s, a decade after the dot com boom, the fashion industry, like many other industries, experienced a second wave of digital innovation. Web 2.0 was a rush by brands to catch up to mobile apps and social media, and digitally native brands took full advantage of the disruption in the industry. Third Love and Lively took market share from Victoria's Secret, and celebrities like Rihanna and Kylie Jenner built beauty empires through social media. However, something has been missing in both waves of internet shopping, and customers are craving inspiration and human contact.

Traffic on mobile has now surpassed traffic on desktop. Global mobile traffic in 2021 was 56 percent, compared to desktop's 44 percent (Bianchi 2023). Shoppers may ultimately make their purchase on a website, but there is a reason why the hashtag #TikTokMadeMeBuyIt is so popular. And the TikTok platform, like Instagram and Facebook before it, is rapidly introducing new features to drive more in-app buying (Lebow 2022).

The lack of human connection in a web store has allowed social apps to fill that void. And this brings me back to the immersive internet, Web 3.0. What if shopping online could be inspirational and feel more natural? What if shoppers could slow down, digitally try on clothes, and even communicate with someone on the other end?

Some experts believe, and I agree, that today's internet, which evolved from a decade of dot coms to a decade of mobile apps, has been evolving to reach a place where the fashion industry was always meant to be: Web 3.0. When we were building the dot com for a legacy retailer, we requested features and functionality that were not possible at that time. But a 3D internet, which will soon be a reality, takes things way beyond what we were asking for.

My first time in a metaverse experience in 2021 was unlike anything I, or my colleagues on the original Saks dot com team, could ever have imagined; I will delve more deeply into this experience later. The Metaverse, as part of Web 3.0, promises to be an immersive and visual internet. It will provide a digital experience that, as we've learned from the virtual gaming industry, brings back the fun of shopping, whether alone or with others.

The Metaverse doesn't exist yet. But, the era is fast approaching, perhaps in this decade, where browsing and inspiration can happen in the same way they can in physical stores. As we've seen before, these evolutions take time. We can see elements of Web 3.0 today, but as a whole new connected internet, it will be some years away.

Matthew Ball eloquently describes the components that must evolve and advance to bring the Metaverse to fruition in terms of networks, computing power, graphics engines, and cutting-edge hardware (Big Think 2022). And then, of course, mass adoption by users is required, which has not been an issue during past internet disruptions. Investors are funneling substantial amounts of money into making it happen. As McKinsey reported in 2022, $120 billion in investments flowed into the Metaverse, and they predict its market impact will be up to $5 trillion by 2030 (McKinsey & Company 2022).

At first, the idea of the Metaverse felt like nothing more than a concept. And in reality, it *is* just a concept. It was impossible to imagine what it could feel like until I inevitably entered a metaverse experience myself. When I became an avatar and started exploring beautiful virtual spaces, I discovered some apps also provided avatars and immersive experiences, and I could enter one the way I did on a website.

Perhaps the future of tech sounds near-dystopian. I want to better explain what's to come so readers understand how the next era of the internet will actually be more humanlike and more natural than today's internet. And we will feel more connected and understood than once imagined. In my quest to unravel my pressing questions about this new realm, I encountered many others who shared similar inquiries and experienced the same lack of answers. It's natural to feel confusion and skepticism about a major disruptive force with much hype but not much visible traction.

I wrote this book to bring clarity about this virtual realm, highlight some possibilities that can fulfill the market predictions, and even recommend where to start. The Metaverse is predicted to have a market impact on every industry by the end of this decade, especially e-commerce. Business owners and corporate leaders alike will benefit from learning the basics of using this immersive internet to connect with consumers. In fact, one study estimates the biggest impact by far from the Metaverse will be on e-commerce, with a potential market impact of $2 trillion to $2.6 trillion by 2030 (McKinsey & Company 2022).

To solidly understand how this can be, I have spent countless hours researching and interviewing experts to combine my learning with my experience as a merchant and veteran in the industry. The consumer desire for fashion in the Metaverse is inevitable, and you can see the evidence in gaming, the online behaviors of the next generations, and the early traction of the luxury market.

My research will highlight evidence of what the fashion consumer craves—brand inspiration, outfit inspiration, human connectivity, and the ability to try on merchandise and receive feedback about their options. I will show how, historically, these components have been missing from online shopping. But the Metaverse promises the next era of the internet will fill these needs like never before, and gaming is giving us a glimpse. Luxury brands never really embraced the dot com era, but they are jumping in with two feet for Web 3.0.

Brands can choose to wait and scramble later, as many brands did in the Web's first and second eras. History tells us this is a costly decision. Or, brands can prepare sooner and take advantage of the massive opportunity for the early adopters who are ready to step into the Metaverse when the technology unleashes its full potential.

PART I

THE WHY OF WEB 3.0, THE METAVERSE, AND FASHION

CHAPTER 1

DISCOVERING THE METAVERSE

I think what you've just been through is a small warm up for what we're now on the brink of. And we didn't even get it right on the warm up.

—SAM ALTMAN, TECH ENTREPRENEUR AND CEO, OPENAI

THE INEVITABLE NEXT EVOLUTION OF THE WEB

I wake up and pick up my phone. Immediately, I click on the weather app and then click on the radar to see the green blanket of rain over the island of Manhattan, happy to see that it is just about to pass north to Connecticut. As I put on my running gear, I open up my missed texts from last night, including one that links to a sweater I've had on my wish list for quite a while, which is now on sale.

I put my Bluetooth headphones on, buy the sweater with a couple more taps, tap on my Spotify running playlist, and head out the door. The dance beat of the electronic dance music (EDM) I curated is exactly what I need to get me going. After hearing the last song on my playlist, I'm blessed with a new song I've never heard before, and I love it. The artificial intelligence that selected it for me was on the mark. I immediately tap the plus sign to "favorite" it and add it to my chosen playlist, ensuring I will hear it again tomorrow.

Prior to 2008, with the advent of mobile apps, none of this was possible to do on a phone. Before streaming music, which was revolutionary, we relied on the iPod, a device that itself was life-changing for many.

I will never forget the first time I laid my eyes on an iPod. In late spring of 2003, I was on a plane headed to the resort towns of Italy and the South of France when corporate jets were still a thing, and my colleagues and I were traveling to get "inspiration" for next season's trends. This was the one annual trip in which our CEO would bring along her husband and son, who was twelve years old at the time.

Because she traveled so much, she always liked to get her son the coolest gifts she could find. On this trip, he was holding a shiny white object—the size of a thick calculator but with no buttons. None of us had ever seen anything like it before.

When he said, "It holds a thousand songs," my eyes almost popped out of my head, and I had to hold it in my own hands.

For this trip, I had packed my own MP3 player, onto which I had downloaded the maximum fifteen-song playlist. Creating and editing the playlist and uploading it to the MP3 player was always a production, but it was worth it. The idea of having a device that could hold one thousand songs and endless playlists was incomprehensible to me. In my gut, I felt an extraordinary excitement about all the possibilities this new "iPod" could bring. Having that much music with me on a run would ensure I would never get bored with one playlist again.

One year after getting my hands on my first iPod, I went from running no more than six miles at a time to training for a marathon—and surpassing every fitness goal I had ever had. It was life-changing.

Although I clearly remember the shift to the iPod, I don't remember the moment I started using my phone for music, or the first time I placed a mobile order for clothing. It was a gradual and seamless evolution. The era of mobile and apps is referred to as Web 2.0, but that is not part of our everyday language. And most people don't have a strong recollection of how we shifted our time from desktop to mobile apps. People didn't all join Facebook or Instagram on the same day. They gradually joined a platform because others were on it. It was the continuous advancement of networks and devices that ultimately transformed our behaviors.

A transition to the Web 3.0 era will likely happen the same way; some are calling today's internet Web 2.5. Just by going to Snapchat, anyone can turn the camera to selfie mode and apply a filter that turns their hair fuchsia, adds virtual earrings, or turns their whole self into a talking cartoon version of themselves. This is called augmented reality, which is a feature of Web 3.0, even if no one on Snapchat calls it that.

Web 3.0 consists of many interrelated pieces, but when I started learning about this thing called *The Metaverse*[1], my curiosity took over, and I went all in. Every book or article I read and every podcast I listened to was from the outside looking in. I decided that to really understand the Metaverse, I needed to experience a virtual world from the inside.

---

[1] A note about capitalizing the word Metaverse. When I refer to the proper "Metaverse," the way we refer to the World Wide Web, I will capitalize it, as that refers to a new channel of the internet that will be immersive and connected, as one ecosystem. When I use it to describe an immersive virtual world, the way we would use the word website, I will use lowercase "metaverse." This is somewhat controversial because it's not possible to have plural metaverses, but there are immersive virtual worlds that one enters with an avatar, referred to as metaverse worlds or experiences.

THE METAVERSE MOMENT

Within minutes of creating my avatar and stepping into a virtual world in early 2022, I felt the same excitement as when I first held an iPod that could hold one thousand songs. I originally thought I'd need to buy a virtual reality (VR) headset, but I was glad to learn it's not required. I announced to my partner where I was going, and then went to my desk behind closed doors and turned on my big monitor.

To start, I needed to make an avatar. I wanted one that could go into different metaverse worlds, so I researched and went to Ready Player Me to create it. At first, it felt a little like making a bitmoji, where you choose your eyes, hair, outfit, and so on. But it was different. It was three-dimensional. And it moved. It went places. I chose a spiky bobbed hairstyle in hot pink, the same hair color I have on my Netflix profile, and it was fun to snap on different virtual outfits until I found a patent leather coat dress with knee-high puffer boots that seemed to fit my personality—even inspiring me to consider a similar look in real life.

My next step was to choose a metaverse world to explore. After some research, I decided on Spatial.io, a metaverse platform known for its culture and whose investors include a coinventor of the Macintosh and a cofounder of Instagram. Intrigued by its reputation, I eagerly set out to embark on my virtual adventure.

Upon entering Spatial, I was pleasantly surprised that I could easily import my existing avatar—no need to start from scratch to create a new digital version of myself. It was an instant connection. Walking around in virtual reality as an avatar was an experience like nothing I had ever encountered. I was not an avid video gamer, so I never had a need for a moving avatar before.

As I began my metaverse journey, it was quite simple to set up my own place—a stunning, modern home with majestic mountain views and twenty-foot ceilings, blush-pink walls, and an expansive outdoor terrace offering breathtaking panoramic views of mountains and glistening water that seemed to go on forever. It was a personal sanctuary that nicely reflected my tastes and desires within this immersive new world.

With my virtual haven in place, I ventured out to explore the wonders Spatial had to offer, and my curiosity led me to the Vogue Singapore gallery. Entering the pristine showcase, I was captivated by the wall installations. These larger-than-life creations evoked a sense of wonder, and I was mesmerized by the creativity showcased within this virtual realm.

I ventured deeper, past a collection of futuristic mannequins elegantly dressed in gravity-defying gowns, their ethereal beauty defying the laws of physics. Compelled to get a closer look at the captivating photography adorning the walls, I approached a particularly intriguing image of a model donning an elaborate headdress. To my astonishment, what I had initially assumed to be a colorful photograph turned out to be a three-dimensional digital artwork inside a frame. The subject within it seemed to come alive, morphing and transforming into avant-garde art before my eyes—an enchanting mix of technology and artistic expression.

When I went back to look at the gown display, I was surprised to learn that as one of the first fifty attendees to this show, I had the privilege of selecting one of the showcased dress styles as a memento to bring back with me. And indeed, it later showed up in my virtual closet, which was a pleasant reminder of my first journey in this immersive realm.

As I leisurely roamed through other virtual buildings, I found myself among the presence of other avatars, but I kept to myself, relishing the artwork, architecture, and even the simulated nature landscapes that surrounded me. It had been a mere fraction of an hour, yet the exhilaration I felt was reminiscent of the awe I experienced over two decades ago when I first encountered an iPod capable of storing a thousand songs. The possibilities flooded my imagination, and I could easily understand how the younger generations found immense joy within these virtual worlds. It was easy to envision so many ways this digital frontier could completely disrupt how we spend our time, connect with others, and, particularly, how we engage in the act of commerce.

Wandering through this immersive three-dimensional world, a sense of fulfillment washed over me. It was more gratifying than mere screen time spent looking at art or nature on a flat surface or through a video. It was much more immersive, and it captured my attention. And although I hesitated to engage with strangers, the presence of fellow avatars around me was a comforting reminder that I was not alone on this journey. In fact, the thought of encountering familiar faces sometime in the future reassured me that I would feel compelled to stay awhile in this wild new realm.

In that profound moment, it struck me. If shops within this virtual expanse existed, offering an array of clothing and accessories for my avatar, then I could imagine indulging in a newfound passion for virtual fashion. The allure of expressing my avatar's style and persona through digital clothing ignited an excitement within me, amplifying the potential of this evolving Metaverse as a virtual shopping destination.

At that precise instant, I realized I was witnessing the dawn of a new technological era—one that held immense promise for fashion in the online realm. I had a flashback as I recalled the challenges we faced when building that first dot com venture from the ground up, and the limitations imposed by the developers, based on what was possible then. Yet now, hope emerged, and it seemed that this new virtual landscape, in this new version of the Web, could finally mirror the seamless nature of shopping in a way that feels organic and intuitive.

Filled with a renewed sense of wonder, I continued to explore, but I couldn't contain my excitement. I picked up my laptop and looked for my partner in the other room. I was eager to share the discovery of this extraordinary new world and my new digital identity, and I couldn't wait to tell everyone else I knew.

VALIDATION OF VIRTUAL WORLDS
My foray into a metaverse world via Spatial.io was a moment I will always remember, but I'll also remember that as captivating as it was, the rendering didn't look very photorealistic. As I pondered that fact, it occurred to me that a real-time 3D experience requires much more technology than an audio file of a song. A few weeks later, I was on a Zoom call with the CEO of a well-known fashion brand, and I asked her what her thoughts about the Metaverse were.

"Why should I care about the Metaverse if my customers aren't there?" she quickly blurted out.

She had a point. There were not many people when I went in then, nor are there many people—a year later—when I visit other "metaverse" worlds like *Decentraland* and *The Sandbox*.

For many people and business leaders, it can be difficult to understand how the Metaverse can be anything beyond video games because the focus of virtual reality has been on gaming for decades. But it's important to understand why the validation for the Metaverse can be seen *in* those gaming worlds.

For many people, the appeal of the internet is to connect with others, and for many gamers, that's the same appeal. For example, one of the most successful games in the world, *Fortnite* by Epic Games, was a *one-player* shooting game when first released in 2017, and it was not a smash hit. When it updated a year later to a "Battle Royale" mode that friend groups could play in and compete with one hundred players, it became one of the most-played games on the planet. By 2021, it had four hundred million registered users, generating $5.8 billion in annual revenue (Boulevard 2022; Iqbal 2023).

Clearly, the appeal of connecting with others versus playing alone was a major factor in *Fortnite's* popularity. So much so that Epic Games added a "Party Royale" mode where there's no shooting, just hanging out in nonviolent contexts (Stevenson 2020). Gamers also care how they look as their virtual selves, and they spend money on that, but we'll get to that later. For younger generations, gaming is their social platform. Even if, in later years, they lose interest in playing video games, they will already be comfortable with a digital identity and being in virtual spaces.

As we will see later in this book, gamers are spending currency and dressing their avatars to hang out with others and explore virtual worlds. In some video games, like *Call of Duty,* the avatars and environment look very realistic. But with that high-level rendering, just as in *Fortnite,* there is a limit to how many players can be in a game at a time. The rendering is also at a higher level when played on a console or with a graphics card inserted into a computer.

For the Metaverse to draw in the masses, the technology and rendering will have to advance, and, unlike games that limit the number of players, it will have to accommodate billions of people in real time, which is still some years away. Web 1.0 and Web 2.0 have been incredible for advancing so much of what we can do in our everyday lives, from the internet to mobile apps and streaming, but technology is always evolving, and there are many new trends today that validate and give us glimpses that the internet is headed to Web 3.0.

TECHNOLOGY AND INNOVATION TRENDS

Today's technology trends are advancing at unprecedented speed, and Web 3.0 will integrate them. For example, augmented reality has turned Snapchat from a teen social media app into a camera filter technology that is being adopted by numerous partners, from Nike to Cartier, for anyone to use on the Snap app. Augmented reality (AR) is also being used by the military for training exercises, and it's being used for spinal surgeries at Johns Hopkins (Ball 2022, 229).

Virtual reality (VR), through advancements in technology and networking, helped gaming grow into an almost $200 billion industry (the global TV market is $259 billion), and it is expected to grow by 50 percent in the next five years (Takahashi 2022). Virtual reality is used to train pilots to fly and to build smart airports with a virtual digital twin that enables scenario planning and security (Ball 2022, 35, 75).

Virtual reality and the Metaverse entered many people's radars when Facebook changed its name to Meta in 2022. Digital collectibles—non-fungible tokens, or NFTs—are made possible because of the blockchain, which is another emerging technology we will discuss in a later chapter (Rojas 2022). Artificial intelligence exploded in November 2022 when ChatGPT launched. It reached one hundred million users in sixty days. The second closest app to that speed was TikTok, and it took nine months (Hu 2023).

Artificial intelligence is the reason why we are closer than we think to having the Metaverse in our daily lives. AI makes progress exponentially faster, and the speed with which it is progressing is mind-blowing.

The power of generative AI has revolutionized the creation of avatars and environments, reducing the time required from days to mere seconds (Velasquez 2023). This has led two of the world's largest companies, Microsoft and NVIDIA, to team up in 2023 to create an industrial metaverse platform. This breakthrough technology will enable digital replicas of facilities and people and real-time 3D collaboration, which can extend to any industry (NVIDIA 2023). For many companies that use Microsoft products, their employees' first avatar experience may start in the workplace very soon.

I heard one inspiring story when I met the talented Lior Cole. She was a computer science student at Cornell University, on a break in New York City, when a talent scout discovered her and she started modeling for designers like Louis Vuitton.

During intervals between fashion shows, she honed her knowledge and acquired cutting-edge tech skills by consuming online tutorials and YouTube videos. At age twenty-two, she is pushing boundaries and running an AI start-up she founded at the intersection of AI and fashion. How did she accomplish this so fast? "The best way to learn something is firsthand experience with it." She sees how technology removes barriers because "humans are not good at the execution part, but they're good at the creative part… so why should a person learn to write code? Learn what the code should say, then have the AI write it."

All of these Web 3.0 technology trends—artificial intelligence, augmented reality, virtual reality, and the blockchain—escalated during the pandemic in 2020, rapidly evolved, and will be integrated into the Metaverse. The innovation that is the Metaverse is already progressing across many industries, as we saw above, not just fashion and retail. It may not end up being called the Metaverse, but regardless of the name, the next internet era will be a 3D immersive internet as a connected virtual ecosystem.

The Metaverse matters because it represents the natural progression of the Web, and every industry will be affected. For brands, it will be a new channel for commerce and connecting, and it will feel more natural than the internet we have today. Technology innovation leads to commerce innovation. It has only been a couple of decades since the World Wide Web led to many breakthroughs that most of us take for granted, like streaming music and movies, social media, and of course, online shopping. It bears repeating Sam Altman once more when he said our current internet is only a "warm-up" of what's to come and "we didn't get it right" the first time. In the next chapter, we'll take a look at the current state before we dive into the future.

CHAPTER 2

ONLINE SHOPPING—WHAT HAS BEEN MISSING?

Today, we experience the internet as "witnesses"... We visit a website to look at it and what it offers. In the Metaverse? We will evolve to experience and engagement.

—RICHARD KERRIS, VP DEVELOPER RELATIONS, NVIDIA

In a split second, two women wearing identical caramel-colored sweatsuits have instantly snapped into chalk-white, cut-out, strappy, long dresses. It is a TikTok post by influencer Denise Mercedes and her best friend, one a size large and the other a small, where she shows their outfit changes to her over three million followers. This ten-second TikTok video is one of many other similar videos with over one million views. The hashtag #Outfitchange, which exploded during the pandemic, already has 6.5 billion views on TikTok.

Since Instagram launched in 2010, people have posted four hundred million "outfit of the day" (#OOTD) hashtags, turning countless people, like Arielle Charnas, into famous influencers with millions of followers. That amounts to *one hundred thousand #OOTD posts per day*. As a comparison, most fashion magazines have less than a thousand pages per month.

During the pandemic, Carla Rockmore, an over-fifty-year-old woman with a massive closet of vintage fashion, asked her son to teach her how to make YouTube videos, leading her to other social media channels. In two short years, she amassed 340,000 YouTube subscribers and 1.3 million on TikTok, and they all love watching her styling tips (Gentry 2023). The numbers say it all: for billions of people, fashion is entertainment, especially "outfits," and it's the ultimate form of self-expression.

People have always loved viewing fashion looks and "fits"—as outfits are often called. The difference is that the gratification is more frequent and much faster now. We've all seen the glossy two-page fashion spreads in *Vogue* and *Elle* magazines and high fashion windows with mannequin presentations made to look like art installations that change every week. These are still just as entertaining as ever, but unlike on social media, they are not in the palm of our hand for entertainment whenever the mood strikes us. Once Instagram came onto the scene, influencers inspired fashion enthusiasts with their outfits, often leading them to make purchases.

The mobile channel and social apps are the foundation of Web 2.0, the internet era we have been in for the past decade. But even Facebook didn't recognize its importance at first. They continued to run their platform as facebook.com and were slow to perfect Facebook's app version. When Instagram launched its app, it had twenty-five thousand users by the end of the first day, one hundred thousand in the first week, and one million in less than three months. This jump led Mark Zuckerberg to buy them out for $1 billion just two years later, in 2012 (History Computer Staff 2022). Vox considers this move "one of the best tech acquisitions of all time, helping secure Facebook's dominance in social media for years to come" (Ghaffary and Heath 2022).

Web 1.0 was a technological revolution, and even a big player like Facebook was slow to realize that mobile apps, Web 2.0, would define the next decade.

TikTok, which launched in 2016, surpassed three billion mobile downloads worldwide by 2021, quickly gaining in popularity and catching up to Facebook and Instagram (Chan 2021). With the hashtag #TikTokMadeMeBuyIt getting 61 billion views as of July 2023, up from 29 billion in December 2022, TikTok has become a shopping phenomenon. And they are still rapidly growing. While Facebook's parent, Meta, has been laying off thousands of people (Paul 2023), TikTok is building a commerce organization, with over one thousand job openings containing the keyword "commerce" as of 2023, according to LinkedIn.

What is social media's, especially TikTok's, draw for shoppers? It fills the void of what's missing from online shopping.

WEB 1.0

So, what is missing from Web 1.0's e-commerce? The shift from brick-and-mortar shopping to online shopping was revolutionary in many ways, but it lacked several key factors—a human connection, outfits, and inspiration.

Rather than seeing a stylist or sales associate, we see a grid of item images as we scroll through pages and pages of styles. Many of us can recall the early days of online shopping on desktops, hours after all stores were already closed, typing something like "denim jacket" into a search bar and magically getting over twenty options to choose from. It's no wonder many in the retail industry soon witnessed the dramatic shift in revenue coming from the online channel, a testament to the incredible convenience of e-commerce. Though that shift escalated with the pandemic, the online experience has not changed much from the early 2000s when most shopping sites initially launched.

As consumers, we search for an item, or we are led there by an email or an ad, then we scroll and browse and scroll some more, sometimes leading to a transaction. Rarely are we entertained at a dot com. Rarely do we have contact with another human being at a dot com, and if we do, it is through a text chat. Little inspiration exists, and no one is showing us how to put outfits together.

Why does the experience lack a human element? Because the Web 1.0 internet was never designed for shopping. Universities and government agencies created the World Wide Web for research and collaboration and designed it to read like a newspaper, i.e., as an "Information Superhighway."

To this day, the world's most premium fashion brands—Hermes, Chanel, Fendi, and so on—do not embrace the current internet as a shopping channel. Although they are active content producers on social media, it took a pandemic for many of them to make their brand websites somewhat shoppable, if at all. A recent study of luxury shoppers by the NN/Norman Neilsen Group found that luxury brand websites are not such a user-friendly experience. These sites tend to suffer from "poor organization and information architecture, few photos of the product… missing product details… and sloppy UI design and bugs" (Moran 2022).

When the internet arrived, most fashion brands eventually embraced a digital transformation. However, most *luxury* brands have barely advanced their website usability in the past twenty years.

I remember being a young executive on the team that launched SaksFifthAvenue.com. One aspect of my job was to convince these luxury brands to be part of our online apparel merchandise assortment when we launched. From our end, it was critical to have the same "fashion authority" online as we did in brick-and-mortar stores.

A typical appointment went something like this: My boss and I arrived to meet the brand executives at the plush showroom in midtown Manhattan with full ammunition in hand. They had yet to create a website of their own, but we brought large, full-color, printed images of our site's pages that were a work in progress. Our creative director and user experience (UX) designers prepared mock-ups of what a potential brand page would look like, including a special landing page, complete with the brand's imagery and logo.

After excitedly pitching our vision for this imminent web era, the questions came.

"How will we be differentiated?"

"How can you create a boutique for us?"

"So when someone searches, the default is that all price points and brands mix together?"

And then their answer: "No, our ready-to-wear cannot be on your website."

Secretly, I couldn't entirely blame them. We had just spent about nine months building the web baby we planned to give birth to. In the beginning, we had full-day meetings in a conference room, with many of the seats filled by an external team of people we collaborated with to build the site. There were web developers and designers, workflow experts, project managers, our chief operations officer—an ex-McKinsey consultant—and me—the merchandising expert.

At one of our first internal meetings to discuss the vision for the site, I arrived with enough experience doing business with these luxury brands to know what they expected. I described in detail what the dot com experience would need to be for our premium collection partners. I gave details about a visual and enticing boutique-like experience where we could highlight all the brand's prestyled "looks" to make the customer feel like she was viewing a runway. There were to be no "grid of items" in the premium designer "boutique."

Time and again, the external team shot me down with, "That is not how e-commerce works." A debate ensued for some time, and it continued to come up daily every time we encountered the next page template to design.

How would we differentiate the shopping experience if we couldn't design something different from the same grid Amazon used to sell books?

We heard the word "No" time after time from the tech team; therefore, it wasn't a total surprise when we heard "No" again from the luxury brand executives themselves.

Again, the design of the World Wide Web was for research, and primarily, that is how organizations used it in the 1970s and 1980s. In 1994, a report that provided the blueprint for the "evolution of the information superhighway" was released with the title "Realizing the Information Future: The Internet and Beyond" (Leiner 2022). It was literally designed to provide information.

But that same year, someone brilliantly turned the information superhighway into commerce—as a marketplace for books.

Jeff Bezos opened Amazon for business in 1995. He was packing boxes from his garage in Bellevue, Washington, to ship to the early adopters of the internet, who were brave enough to put their credit card information online. Many people had reservations at first, and the term Cyber Monday wasn't coined until 2005 (Webley 2010). Though Amazon started with books, it gradually added many more categories, and twenty years later, there are few categories that it *doesn't* sell.

When set up properly, with excellent attributing and navigation, an e-commerce site is an amazing tool for searching. And convenience and speed—for the most part. Online shopping is not the most pleasant place to browse, and it certainly isn't a place we usually shop with friends. Twenty years after the day we went live with saks.com, I do buy many of my clothes online, as do most people I know.

I miss the days when shopping meant an entire Saturday spent with a best friend. Even ten years ago, I would meet my BFF for our seasonal full day of shopping on New York's Fifth Avenue. We'd try clothes on for each other to give our opinions and separate our tried-on items into three piles—keep, maybe, and no way. We would add everything up at the end to see the total damage, often thrilled with everything we picked out, knowing we'd return none of it.

Online shopping is certainly more convenient, especially when you know what you want, but it does not compare to knowing how it looks when it's on.

Online shopping is missing more than just the touch and feel of fabrics and trying clothes on. It's missing the inspiration you get when you walk through a gorgeous store with displays that tell a story about the brand's collection or a trend, the outfit ideas, and the emotional support of a good friend or associate who will give you an honest opinion about the outfit you're trying on. It's no wonder that ten years later, a disruptive force emerged as Web 2.0.

WEB 2.0

Right around the ten-year mark of e-commerce, we seamlessly entered Web 2.0. This is the era we are in now. We have shifted to Mobile and Social. Like most people, on a typical day, when I turn on my phone, I end up visiting a social media app. Today, I saw a feed on Instagram from Neiman Marcus with a pleated skirt I am ready to purchase. On another day, I saw an outfit on an influencer that I could "picture myself in."

It's called "social" media, but when it comes to the shopping experience on social media, it sure feels like these conversations are very one-sided for most of us. It feels more like "stalker" media.

Influencers comprise less than 5 percent of social media users. I calculated this with the statistic that fifty million people globally considered themselves influencers in 2022 (Gagliese 2022). The world population is eight billion, and Instagram, for example, has two billion active monthly users (Worldometer. n.d.; Ruby 2023). So even if there were now one hundred million influencers on Instagram, that is still less than 4 percent of the app's users. This means over 95 percent of us are merely "observers/followers."

As followers, we can build community and socialize with other users and even some influencers. But, for the most part, we are observing and reacting—usually alone. Live events bring people together for shopping, but socially, it is not the same as going to a physical store with a friend. We may use social media apps to share content with our connections, but when it comes to fashion, it is not really a "social" thing.

In terms of shopping for fashion, Web 1.0 was a revolution in the convenience it brought to our lives. It was efficient and transactional, but it lacked the qualities of human connection, inspiration for outfits, and differentiated brand experiences. Web 2.0 brought us, in many ways, shopping as inspiration and entertainment—from influencers, from brands, and from stores. Viral videos of "outfit changes" provide a way to imagine how a look might appear on us.

That in itself is a massive improvement even from physically shopping in a store—where we have to sift through clothing racks and edit down to what we are willing to try on. It takes work to decide what we will try on and effort to put it on. So it's no wonder why the hashtags

#OOTD and #GRWM—get ready with me—are so popular. People love to see fashion looks, even if someone else is trying them on.

So, with all that outfit inspiration, what is missing from Web 2.0? We are not choosing the outfits to see because the influencers are. We may find influencers that we identify with and can "imagine" how the fashion may appear on us. But they are not us. And as "social" as it may be called, we are usually observing alone.

Namisha Jain, a Boston Consulting Group consultant who researches consumers and what they want when they go shopping, reminisced about her college years during her TEDx Talk about conversational commerce:

My friends and I would spend a few hours every month on "Fashion Street," a euphemism for the row of small stores with the latest clothes at great prices. We would spend hours rummaging through piles of clothes, trying on dozens of trinkets, and getting advice from each other on what looked good and what was on trend.

She loves the fast-growing Chinese conversational shopping platform, Pinduoduo, because

It's lonely to shop online, and I miss hanging out with my friends. But on Pinduoduo, when I find a product, I can either buy it myself at the regular price, or I can share it with my friends via social media, discuss it with them, get their advice, and if we all choose to buy it together, we get a great deal (Jain 2021).

Shopping online is indeed a lonely way to shop, and dot coms are designed to show us *items*, not how to put together an outfit—even though we may love searching on websites for something specific. Social media apps have done a great job of showing us fashion "looks" on influencers, or content creators, who engage us in an entertaining way and inspire us with *outfits*.

Conversational commerce, like the Pinduoduo platform, is an attempt at combining the two. But even more compelling is the next evolution of shopping, in Web 3.0, which will be about seeing the outfits *we* choose on our digital selves. It will also allow us to model those looks for friends or family, as we do in a physical store.

Web 3.0 promises to make the shopping experience feel more like real life. It is being created with a completely new three-dimensional standard, not unlike gaming or what we see from Pixar (The Economist 2022). I spoke with Sasha Wallinger, who worked at Nike when they first experimented with gaming type software. She believes, "the consumer has been bored, but they're not stupid… they're really wanting some stimulation in new, exciting ways."

The insatiable appetite that people show for outfit changes on social media clearly shows she has a point. Because, ultimately, clothing makes people (Lewis 2012). Clothing is not just for utility, but rather, it is the way we express ourselves. In the next chapter, we will explore the significance of self-expression through clothing and delve into how gaming validates the immense power of virtual worlds as platforms for limitless self-expression.

CHAPTER 3

SELF-EXPRESSION

When we dress ourselves we are telling a story every day about our identity, we are curating every day. And the digital space will allow for even richer narratives where we will create wardrobes that are going to be unlimited.

—ADRIANA HOPPENBROUWER-PEREIRA,
CO-FOUNDER, THE FABRICANT

Walking through the spectacular Dior exhibit at the Brooklyn Museum, I stopped short with delight at a photograph of a model posing in front of an ornate mirror in a grand Parisian salon. She was wearing a voluminous white tulle strapless gown, with large rosettes on one hip. This exact image had once been a poster in my bedroom when I had just arrived in New York City at the age of twenty-one. I woke up to that image every day. I would imagine that one day, when I met the right person, I would find a wedding gown inspired by that dress.

Five years later, I was shopping for that perfect dress. It was a frustrating process because I knew what I was looking for, but nothing I tried on even came close. I didn't look good in full skirts, but I wanted the dramatic look from the Dior poster. My idea was to find a fitted lace column with a tulle overskirt that wrapped around the back, leaving the front flat. This dress was the most important dress I would ever wear, and I was not going to settle. When I got to Kleinfeld, the last salon on my list, they did not have anything close to my dream dress—but I was ecstatic when they offered to make a custom gown.

In the New York City garment center, I bought seven large rosettes, one large and the rest in diminishing sizes. The Kleinfeld dream-weavers placed them around the back of the final creation: a sleeveless fitted lace column with a Sabrina neckline and V back. A graceful tulle overskirt wrapped around the back, seamlessly attached by invisible hook-and-eyes, allowing the front of the dress to retain its flat appearance. With the delicate rosettes sewn on, I slipped into the dress, and felt like it exuded romance, confidence, drama, and everything I had hoped.

SELF-EXPRESSION CHALLENGES

At times, we find ourselves yearning to magically bring to life the garments we envision wearing. The world of custom-made clothing, however, has remained out of reach for most of us. Yet, a shift is on the horizon, propelled by the advent of a virtual realm, generative AI, and our new digital identities. In the upcoming digital era of virtual reality, we will be able to craft looks to our exact desires, and they will flawlessly fit us.

Clothing is the primary way most people express their individuality, and stores are full of options. But, most of us struggle to find the items that truly satisfy, and only love a fraction of what is in our closets. When we choose our clothes, we have many boxes we hope to check—how it looks, how it fits, and our desire to look relevant. It's no wonder the hashtag #personalstylist has 3.5 million posts on Instagram, and most celebrities employ their services.

Merchandising, the art and science of predicting the products that customers want, relies on data, but the data can only predict based on the past and present. As a merchant, I'm acutely aware that store assortments are always missing items that could spark joy for customers. The task of identifying those elusive items is no easy feat, but when accomplished, it can signify a tremendous future trend with commercial potential.

Search functionality has helped uncover some of those hidden gems, but often customers' search terms don't match the terms in the database, or they're unsure how to describe them. At times, their desires might be more about expressing themselves through a general aesthetic or trying to solve a pain point relating to fit. Still, different people use different words to describe similar desires.

To navigate these opportunities, an effective approach I've utilized is to analyze customer reviews of items that have sold extremely well, to understand the language they are using to describe the items they love. During a consulting engagement with a dress brand that was trying to move the needle on their business, we implemented this strategy. We analyzed the reviews of the top-selling items, internally, while also scrutinizing the top-rated dresses externally in the market. This took place during a time when music festivals were exploding and the "boho chic" trend was captivating the fashion scene.

Some hidden gems started to emerge as we looked for patterns in the language. Certain delicate, ethereal dresses received many positive reviews, with customers frequently describing them as "soft and flowy." However, these same terms were often used to describe dresses that embodied a bohemian style, which was plentiful. Although in aggregate there were multiple dresses that fit the ethereal, but non-bohemian, aesthetic, no single brand offered very many, thus missing out on potential demand.

Connecting the dots on this, we transformed an internal brand with unique dresses catering to an ethereal appeal. It gave us a tremendous competitive advantage and sparked joy for those seeking a softer expression, resulting in significant growth that endured for years. Had we not paid attention to the reviews and deciphered this nuance, the customers may have missed out on the items they wanted, and the business would have missed out on that demand.

People often have reasons for buying what they buy, which are not easily expressed in words. In her book *Dressed: A Philosophy of Clothes*, author Shahidha Bari, a professor of fashion cultures and histories, writes about the "hopes that we harbor" in our own clothes: "We entrust to them the task of concealing our imperfections and showcasing our assets, presenting us from the outside as we will ourselves to be from the inside" (Bari 2020, 40).

Let's consider another case study involving a swimwear brand that dominated the market but had reached a plateau. For the fifth year in a row, the revenue remained steady but flat. We completed a thorough deep dive, which revealed that, despite the brand's reach, millions of potential customers were not choosing to shop at the brand. It became evident that consumers choosing swimwear, which is their most publicly exposed attire, cared about a critical factor that was not adequately expressed through search terms—their level of modesty.

The brand's silhouette choices didn't provide enough options in the two extremes. Many customers either wanted more coverage or they wanted skimpier, unstructured styles beyond the brand's offering. Revamping the silhouettes to better cater to these two extremes, was one of the strategies that helped us double the business in three years. Once again, the focus was on how people wanted to express themselves. In this case, concealing or showcasing for modesty reasons. Even a brand representing a significant portion of the industry can miss opportunities from untapped demand.

Stores and e-commerce sites are overflowing with options, but the customer is turning elsewhere for inspiration. The true extent of the world's hunger for fashion inspiration became apparent with the advent of Instagram in late 2010. In the chapter about Web 2.0, we saw how influencers posted the hashtag #OOTD an astonishing one hundred thousand times per day. One reason for the popularity of this hashtag may be a need to see what's new and relevant. The challenge for the consumer who is following this hashtag, however, is that they are never choosing the outfits they might want to experiment with, nor are they trying them on themselves.

Bari reflects in her book, "Dressing is so hard, it is astonishing that we ever find the courage to keep trying, as we do every day" (Bari 2020, 76).

There is another key reason why dressing is so hard. We may land on a great style that feels like "us," and we may even be able to try it on, but then it doesn't fit right. We can blame that on ready-to-wear. In previous centuries, clothing had to be custom-made.

Today, styles come in a certain set of sizes, even though every human body is unique. It would take hundreds of sizes to accommodate the unique body types we all have. So even when we do discover the perfect outfit that expresses our true selves, we may struggle to find the perfect fit that flatters our unique physique. This often forces us to compromise on less satisfying alternatives. Dressing is indeed hard.

Clothing is the ultimate form of self-expression, but at times, our bodies prevent us from truly achieving the expression we seek to convey. At its core, the desire for clothing stems from our desire to want to feel good in our clothes, feel confident in our bodies, and express our individuality. Simultaneously, many seek inspiration on social media, wanting to feel in sync with what's relevant for the times, or for fear of judgment otherwise. In the realm of digital fashion, we find a remarkable advantage that is not possible in the challenging world of getting dressed. Digital identities will give us the ability to convey our true selves as avatars, unburdened by the frustrations and anxieties entangled by physical fashion choices.

VIRTUAL WORLD SELF-EXPRESSION
In the world of digital fashion, fit is not part of the equation, opening the door to countless possibilities for experimentation and self-expression. Picture a world where you can effortlessly wear any style without fretting over "concealing imperfections" or conforming to a certain "modesty level." While we will still desire physical versions of some outfits, our avatars will empower us to express ourselves freely, unencumbered by concerns about fit and exposure.

Another advantage of avatars is that we are no longer limited by the outfits that the influencers put together. Nor are we forced to see how they look on someone else. With just a click, we can try on as many outfits as we want, and then walk around and see how they feel. Inspiration will surround us as we explore new spaces and new looks on display or on others. To grasp the true potential of avatar fashion, we need only observe the resounding success achieved in the realm of gaming.

In the gaming world, digital "skins" have already become a $50 billion business. By 2030, today's younger generations, who are virtual natives, will start becoming adults, and they will have been buying digital fashion for over a decade.

In some games, skins are collectible and can actually affect how a player can succeed in the game. However, in *Fortnite,* which is free to play, the skins are purely aesthetic, and they don't affect success in playing. Yet, *Fortnite* took in $5.8 billion in 2021 (Iqbal 2023), and an estimated 59 percent of *Fortnite* players' spending is on outfits or characters (Brown 2023). One of the most compelling aspects of *Fortnite* skins, which has contributed to the game's success, is that they provide customization and personalization, which Gen Zers love (Voxburner Content Team 2022).

Roblox offers the closest comparison to what we can expect in the Metaverse because of its multitude of experience choices. When I went into the platform to try on some outfits, I soon realized what my kids have been saying all along about avatar fashion: why dress like yourself when you can have fun being anyone you want? Even though I still went with my favorite pink hair color, I soon changed the style to some ball-shaped pigtails, which felt really fun. From there, I felt compelled to choose a funkier outfit that worked with the hair, rather than something I would normally want to wear.

There is something so freeing about taking on a new identity and exploring a new place. We can imagine how thrilling it will be when technology allows for rendering that will be more photo-realistic and makes us feel even more real.

For some individuals, the Metaverse and embracing a digital identity can instill a confidence and a newfound sense of courage to authentically express who they are. As one *Vogue* editor recounted in a podcast, "Someone I know came out on *Roblox* a year before he came out to his physical friends" (Barry 2022).

Freedom of self-expression is such an important element in Web 3.0 that I devoted an entire chapter to it. As I recounted before, my experience with creating my avatar was the inspiration to dive deep into this space and, ultimately, write a book. Self-expression has always been a driving factor in getting dressed, but we have been somewhat limited by factors like fit, modesty, or others' expectations of how we should present ourselves. The Metaverse and a digital identity promise what gaming is already proving to be true, which is that self-expression will be a freeing, experimental, and fun experience with fashion we never thought we could wear, and a physical being we never thought we could be.

MERCHANDISING FOR THE METAVERSE
In the Metaverse, the synergy between merchandising and the customers' innate desire for self-expression comes alive. Unlike traditional e-commerce, where all items are created equal, the metaverse store embraces the art of storytelling, much like a physical store does. Customers can find the inspiration they crave from outfits that are thoughtfully grouped with compelling narratives or highlighted trends.

In this chapter, I described previous experiences of how my team and I used existing technology and trends to meet the customers where they're at. In the future, we'll have an opportunity to expand our imaginations and ingenuity using Web 3.0 to create products that customers crave.

For example, within the Metaverse, brands and retailers will be able to sell both digital and physical products that are curated. This opens doors to limitless creativity, where customers can choose between dressing their avatars or purchasing the physical versions, or both, enriching their fashion choices and experiences. Both merchandising/buying and visual merchandising will likely play a critical role in this new channel.

The Metaverse enables customers to exponentially be inspired by brands while shopping. An example is the Alo Yoga metaverse store in *Roblox*, where customers can engage in gamified yoga training through Alo Sanctuary. The experience takes place on an island with a meditative and soothing audio track and meditation retreats. The shoppable store includes items such as leggings, tops, and a trucker hat. Brands in the Metaverse can dream up many ways to inspire customers and reach a broader audience without the constraints of time, budget, and other limitations of physical locations (Alo Yoga 2022).

Customization will also be a key advantage of the Metaverse. Leveraging generative AI, customers can potentially see displays curated for their unique desires. Their virtual closets become a window to their tastes, and AI store assistants can enable recommendations based on those preferences.

In this new era where the Metaverse fuses technology and fashion, brands are able to weave immersive narratives, inspire like never before, and celebrate the beautiful art of self-expression through fashion. In the next chapter, we will discover how this is already happening in gaming virtual worlds.

PART II

THE WHAT OF WEB 3.0, THE METAVERSE, AND FASHION

CHAPTER 4

GAMING AND VIRTUAL WORLDS

Most of the factors that make life meaningful are going to be there in virtual worlds. There's no good reason to think that life in VR (virtual reality) will be meaningless or valueless.

—DAVID CHALMERS, PROFESSOR OF PHILOSOPHY AND
NEURAL SCIENCE, NEW YORK UNIVERSITY

In 2011, Mishi McDuff entered a virtual world, for the first time, because she wanted to attend a concert by Texas music artist, Sean Ryan. To enter the virtual world, *Second Life,* she selected a default avatar. She made her way onto the concert floor, and she was shocked to see that the other avatars had taken on all kinds of identities, some even dressed up as characters like gossamer fairies, fierce warriors, or supermodels.

She stuck out as a newbie in a prepackaged outfit. She decided that for her next virtual concert, she wouldn't make that mistake again. Instead, she showed up in a one-of-a-kind polka-dot dress she created for herself in Adobe Photoshop. As she spent more time in *Second Life,* others started to notice her clothes and great sense of style.

Realizing that people were willing to spend money on their digital identities, she launched her own digital fashion business, House of Blueberry. In that launch year, 2015, her digital collection brought in $60,000. The following year, it brought in $1 million. In mid-2022, House of Blueberry expanded into *Roblox,* projected to do $1.8 million in revenue. A digital clothing item might sell for only one dollar, but House of Blueberry has already sold twenty million digital assets.

Fashion brands are now approaching McDuff for collaborations, and she's already collaborated with brands like Natori, Jonathan Simkhai, and others (Jones 2022). Brands that are unfamiliar with the gaming space and whose teams lack 3D digital designers are enlisting the help of those with such digital design skills and expertise in these platforms (Maguire 2022).

CREATIVITY AND INSPIRATION IN VIRTUAL WORLDS

In 2023, the number of active gamers worldwide is 3.1 billion, which represents over one-third of the world's population (Howarth 2023). *Roblox,* a virtual-world platform with over sixty million daily active users and the fourth largest channel on YouTube, partnered with Parsons School of Design on a trend report. They learned from their customers that nearly 75 percent will spend money on digital fashion, and 12 percent spend $50 to $100 each month (Lee 2022). Christina Wootton, vice president of global partnerships at *Roblox,* points out that, long before media and brands caught on to the vast appeal of digital fashion, "Here, [on *Roblox*], millions of people have been connecting, socializing, creating—and expressing themselves through their digital identity and fashion—for over a decade" (Wootten 2022).

McDuff understood the importance of looking good in a virtual world, especially because she met her husband on *Second Life*. She says, "how you present yourself actually matters just as much as how you do in real life, simply because you're forming these social connections" (Maguire 2022). Mishi's business has caught the attention of investors, and she just raised a round of seed funding (Takahashi 2023). But there are also plenty of people creating clothing for fun in virtual worlds.

An interesting statistic from the Parsons/*Roblox* report is, "there are at least two hundred times as many creators designing clothing and accessories on *Roblox* as there are fashion designers creating physical collections in the United States." What is driving this, Wootton describes is "first, community demand and the role that digital identity plays… where people come to be whoever they want to be. And second, the free tools that are easily available… to create and share digital fashion on *Roblox*" … making "self-expression opportunities truly limitless" (Lee 2022).

In February 2023, Ready Player Me, the avatar platform, launched an experimental lab where users can even use generative AI to create customized fashion using only prompts. I tested it out and was impressed at what my request for an "iridescent leather-textured top" produced for me.

Another fascinating result from the report is that 40 percent of those surveyed said self-expression via clothing and accessories in the digital world is *more* important for them than self-expression in the physical world. And 70 percent [said] they get physical style inspiration from dressing their avatars, just as I did when I first dressed my avatar in a black patent dress. According to Wootton, the data confirmed what they had already observed. "We saw lots of similarities in the way digital and physical fashion impact people's confidence and connection with others, and just how important digital fashion is for Gen Z consumers and their self-expression" (Lee 2022).

Understanding what makes a gaming platform like *Roblox* so successful is important to note for anyone in the fashion industry because fashion does play a role; however, it hasn't always been that way in gaming. It's no secret that gaming has always been dominated by action-packed and sometimes violent games that appealed more to boys than girls. One reason for this could be because most game developers were males who created what appealed to them.

As popular as *Fortnite* is, 90 percent of its users are male (Ruby 2023). But back in 1996, female developers created a video game for the first time that was specifically marketed to girls: Mattel's *Barbie Fashion Designer* on CD-ROM. The game, which enabled girls to make their own Barbie clothes, was the top-selling software title of that year, selling more than even Windows 95. Today, girls make up 48 percent of all gamers (Rousseau 2022).

Karli Kloss's innovative world in *Roblox*, Klosette, launched in spring 2023, and it garnered an astounding twenty million visits in its beta form. Klosette's promise is "to give everyone the opportunity to become fashion icons." When I checked it out, I was pleasantly surprised at the inclusive options for realistic body types and shapes, and the move away from *Roblox's* block-shaped avatars. In the Klosette experience, users are empowered to craft unique style statements by curating outfits and presenting them for community voting. This engaging virtual world doesn't just captivate users who want to unleash their creative styling flair, it is just as compelling for users seeking outfit ideas and fashion inspiration.

It's worthwhile to understand how well "fashion" has done in gaming. There isn't very much public information on financial results for fashion, or "skins," in gaming. However, Epic Games, the maker of *Fortnite*, revealed in 2022 that *Fortnite* sold 3.3 million NFL-branded skins in two months, which translates to about $50 million in just one collection of skins in that time period (Tassi 2022). Demand for virtual goods is evident when we note that there were more than 3 billion transactions in *Roblox* in 2022 alone, and creators earned $624 million (D'Angelo 2023). People are spending on their digital identities (Gonzalez-Rodriguez 2022).

Roblox is not actually a game. It is a free platform with millions of virtual worlds and games that users can pop in and out of. A staggering 75 percent of the 9-to-12-year-old population in the US regularly used *Roblox* in the second quarter of 2020 (Ball 2022, 18). Fast-forward to 2030 and this group will be 19-to-22-year-olds who spent a decade navigating virtual worlds. One of the platform's top games, *Royale High*, has been played five billion times and is ranked number five in popularity on the platform. It was created by Callmehbob—a female gamer with no prior experience as a developer.

After ten years of playing other games, at twenty-two, Callmehbob says of *Royale High*: "I created the game I've been wanting to play but couldn't find anywhere." In *Royale High*, you can earn "diamonds" currency by winning a spelling bee, grabbing the right book from your locker, winning a dance contest, or various other challenges you encounter in school or by exploring magical lands (Hill 2021).

In the rule list of the game, players are encouraged to earn the currency, spend it in the shop, and "dress your character to suit your mood and personality." This is worlds away from a shooter game, and it's one of the most successful games on the platform.

But dressing up isn't the only reason for *Roblox's* huge success. One dad who spent time there and wrote about it said, "One of the keys to the platform's success is the ease with which you can invite friends to join you in different virtual worlds or games… at the click of a button. With open chat channels to friends on their phones, my kids are constantly negotiating which game to join" (Hill 2021).

SOCIALIZATION

Socialization isn't just a compelling feature for young people on *Roblox*. Even a warlike video game can provide a sense of community for adult players. Laura Miele is the chief operating officer at Electronic

Arts (EA), but fifteen years ago, she was a young marketing executive at the same company, living in San Francisco. During that time, she loved playing the popular video game *World of Warcraft* with her family members in Southern California. She recounted a related story in her TEDx Talk in 2021.

We would only see each other once a year, but we played Warcraft a lot… It was unbelievable bonding and so much fun. We were truly connected. This was fifteen years ago. Today, this entire family lives in the Bay area close to us. In fact, my sister-in-law is six blocks away from us. And I kid you not, we spent far more time together and were closer and more connected when we were playing World of Warcraft than we are today.

Miele's key takeaways about gaming:

(1) *In today's divisive world, games can be an incredibly effective way of connecting people, even breaking geographic location boundaries.* (2) *Smaller groups and smaller friend groups have incredible holding power for players to continue to engage and keep coming back to the games they love. There are billions of people playing games, but what's most meaningful to players are the small groups they play with every day* (Academy of Interactive Arts & Sciences 2022).

Whether it's kids on *Roblox* or adult family members on *World of Warcraft*, this idea of spending time with smaller friend groups is the same. This is a unique feature of virtual worlds that keeps people coming back for more. It is not possible to meet up with friends on a dot com; though, social media allows friends to chat in groups. But a virtual world provides immersive socialization with activities.

It matters how users show up and what they wear—whether it's playing a game or visiting a magical world. Gaming sometimes gets a reputation for attracting introverts who want to be alone. But, in a recent survey of people who are using virtual platforms that are today's version of the Metaverse, "almost 60 percent… said they were excited about transitioning everyday activities to it, with connectivity among people the biggest driver, followed by the potential to explore digital worlds" (McKinsey & Company 2022).

This virtual connectivity and exploration make it different than any experience in the first two eras of the internet.

The current population of 12-to-24-year-olds—Gen Z—grew up connecting with their friends on platforms like *Roblox* or the highly addictive games of *Minecraft* and *Fortnite*. They have developed strong digital identities and are, therefore, buying fashion in new ways. This generation makes up about 25 percent of the world's population and possesses the unique distinction of being the first true inhabitants of the virtual world. They are the virtual world natives. After all, Wi-Fi didn't even exist until 1997 (Branka 2023).

This unique attribute in the upbringing of Gen Z, combined with their deep immersion in social media, also makes them the most culturally different from preceding generations. The younger individuals in this demographic might not have cash or credit cards, but they have a digital currency that they earn in gaming environments. Surprisingly, they choose to spend it on avatar fashion. Although the exact nature of the Metaverse remains uncertain, the immersive nature of gaming offers a captivating glimpse into the appeal of virtual worlds, where social interactions more closely mirror real-life encounters than the 2D internet.

STATUS

Besides human connectivity, another element of the Metaverse that truly mirrors real life is the desire for status. The reason why some of the most successful brands in the world, which have been around for over a century in some cases, are luxury brands is because people are attracted to status. The virtual world of gaming is no different.

For example, during a virtual event in *Roblox* hosted by Gucci, a virtual Gucci bag sold for $4,115, which is worth more than the physical bag at $3,400 (Ernest 2021). Ralph Lauren, Tommy Hilfiger, Burberry, and Nike have all created digital items in *Roblox*. In the *Roblox*/Parsons survey, two-thirds of the respondents said they are excited for their avatars to wear brand names (Lee 2022).

And it's not just in *Roblox*. In 2021, Balenciaga became the first luxury brand to launch a partnership with *Fortnite* for digital and physical fashion, followed by Moncler (Campbell 2021). Ralph Lauren did the same in 2022 with their Polo brand. Another report found that 64 percent of virtual world gamers agreed that seeing other avatars wearing branded clothing makes them want to wear the brand (YPulse 2023).

Wearing brand names is not the only way to earn status in the Metaverse. Players who achieve high levels in games become celebrities. Collectors of rare NFTs—collectible digital assets—like CryptoPunks flaunt their ownership by using the image as their profile picture (PFP). Virtual real estate—housing, cars, and so on—will have its own worth in the Metaverse.

The longing for status within the virtual realm reflects our innate human nature. Whether in the physical or digital world, the drive for social status is a universal aspect of human behavior that transcends the boundaries of any world we inhabit.

GETTING PRACTICAL

The allure of gaming platforms is evident in their ability to facilitate socializing, activities, dressing up, and even flexing status. But there is also a more practical reason why gaming is closely tied to the future immersive internet. Video games and virtual worlds are built the same way. In fact, every virtual world is built on a game engine, and these engines will be part of the building blocks of the Metaverse.

If you look at a game engine displayed on a computer screen, it resembles a software package similar to Adobe Illustrator and Photoshop. However, no other design software can begin to compare to the complexity of a game engine. It possesses the remarkable ability to build three-dimensional objects and environments utilizing a mesh format while also enabling movement of the objects through these spaces and an infinite number of rules governing actions and reactions. The leading game engines, namely Unreal Engine—owned by Epic Games—introduced in 1998, and Unity, released in 2005, have been advancing for about two decades and are currently extensively utilized in the development of numerous metaverse worlds (Eldad 2023).

As the new era of virtual worlds gets built, retailers, fashion brands, schools, and other organizations will most likely use these engines to build their virtual experiences for commerce, classrooms, events, and so on (Ball 2022, 72). So, even a virtual world that has nothing to do with gaming is still run on an engine that was originally created for gaming.

Unity powers the Spatial virtual world I visited, and it enables creators to build 3D environments. Apple's new Vision Pro headset was also designed in partnership with Unity to accommodate apps made with that engine (Schafer 2023). LVMH is now directly working with the teams at Epic Games's Unreal Engine to build new virtual experiences (Kelly 2023). Understanding the similarities in building these worlds is one more reason why we can learn so much from the gaming industry to understand the future immersive internet.

When we look at the appeal of the gaming world, beyond the actual playing of games, we can see it closely mirrors real life in many ways but in a virtual reality. Users attend activities, connect with others, and express their identities. In gaming worlds, they enjoy the self-expression that digital fashion provides, and they get dressed according to the places they are going, aware of the image they are showing to others with the clothing they choose.

And status is status whether it is in real life or a virtual world. Much of this is new to those of us who are nongamers, but for Gen Z and Gen Alpha, this is the world they know. They may not have an income, but playing to earn is how they get the currency to live out their indulgences and express their identity.

The intersection of gaming, virtual worlds, and fashion offers a unique glimpse into the future of the immersive internet. The Metaverse is indeed a natural progression for the younger generations, who have grown up immersed in digital identities and virtual worlds. However, its potential extends far beyond these demographics. As we recognize the similarities between virtual and real-life experiences, it becomes evident that this immersive internet is poised to reshape our existence on a global scale and in ways we can only begin to imagine.

CHAPTER 5

EXTENDED REALITIES— XR, AR, MR, VR

We as a society—as people—Homo sapiens—did not evolve for thousands of years to interact with 2D interfaces. We didn't evolve to learn by tapping a piece of glass... many believe that the next evolution is 3D experiences.

—MATTHEW BALL, CEO, EPYLLION; AUTHOR, *THE METAVERSE*

On May 26, 2022, ABBA's extraordinary musical event, *Voyage*, described as "Retro Futurism," opened in London. Through revolutionary tech innovation, the band members, who are in their seventies, got on stage together for the first time in forty years, exactly as they were in 1979, though donning a new wardrobe. It wasn't really them but hyperrealistic digital avatars, dubbed "Abbatars," accompanied by a ten-piece live band. They performed their "Chiquititas" and "Fernandos," swaying and swishing their hair the way they do, to a sold-out semi-intimate crowd of three thousand (Empire 2022).

Countless fans were in tears or in jaw-dropping awe, feeling like they had gone back in time (Morris 2022). One fan, Romily Newman, posted her reaction on social media, "Nothing will ever compare. Not my wedding, not the birth of my firstborn, nothing." A reporter from *Esquire* wrote, "The show might be virtual, but the feelings it evokes are genuine. I know, I felt them" (Bilmes 2022). These avatars, not holograms, generated that much emotion during this mind-bending new concert experience, utilizing an invisible 213-foot pixel screen, created with George Lucas's digital effects company, Industrial Light & Magic (ILM).

The costume designer, Bea Åkerlund, who wanted the costumes to "feel disco, yet modern," rather than nostalgic, considered how the four band members would have looked if they had never aged and were performing today. She enlisted Dolce & Gabbana, Manish Arora, known as the "Galliano of India," and others to create looks that ranged from "high-fashion, to fantasy, to futuristic"—enabling twenty costume changes (Maisey 2022).

How was this experience produced? The band members performed the songs for over five weeks and were filmed wearing motion capture suits. Then their "de-aged" avatar physiques were created using body doubles and archival footage. One thousand animators worked on digitizing the 3D footage to be projected on the invisible screen (Borrelli-Persson 2022).

In June 2023, I attended *my* first virtual reality concert. The concert was at The Shed, the avant-garde oasis in New York City, which is a much smaller venue than the spaceship-like arena created for the ABBA show. For this solo piano performance, I sat in a large circle with the other thirty-nine concertgoers, donning a headset, and found myself facing a virtual grand piano under a spotlight, where the late pianist Ryuichi Sakamoto was seated and ready to play. As the dramatic music filled the air, everyone in the audience stood and walked up to the piano, circling around it to experience every angle. Through the headset, we could still see each other, albeit in a dark setting, and got close enough to almost touch the star's nimble fingers dancing on the piano keys—a rare privilege that would never have been possible in real life.

Tech innovations that bring us alternative realities are happening all around us, and people are embracing them. ABBA's Voyage show has been extended for another year because of high demand. These tech trends prepare us for a future where innovations will seamlessly blur digital and physical lines with our online presence. I believe that, for most nongamers, what will bring them into the Metaverse for the first time, if not work-related, will be virtual entertainment, perhaps a concert. These various extended realities (XR) are all part of Web 3.0 and will converge in the Metaverse.

Ryan David Mullens, whom I interviewed for this book, is the former head of innovation at Adidas and the founder and CEO of Aglet, a successful gaming app he launched in 2020. In his take on the state of the Metaverse, he asks us to imagine we're looking at a child about to build a Lego object with all the pieces scattered on the floor. We don't know exactly how it's going to look, but we know all the necessary pieces are there and coming together. Although the Metaverse is still several years away because of technology constraints, we can see these "pieces" just by observing all the cutting-edge technology trends of today, and we will dive into them in this chapter.

Mullens views the digital realm as part of real life and not separate from it, as is evident from his company name, On Life. The game he founded, Aglet, also serves as a fitness tracker, which entices 4.5 million active users to walk outdoors to earn virtual sneakers by arriving at random locations on a real-time GPS map.

Not surprisingly, Aglet has formed partnerships with real brands—from major sneaker brands like Adidas to sports teams in the Premier League. The game sometimes leads the user to physical stores for small rewards, potentially driving additional purchases. Essentially, it's connecting the digital experience to the physical world.

AUGMENTED REALITY

Apple CEO Tim Cook famously said, "Zoom out to the future and look back, you'll wonder how you led your life without augmented reality. Just like, today, we wonder: 'How did people like me grow up without the internet?'" (Huddleston 2022)

Augmented reality (AR) technology, which superimposes a computer-generated image over an object or space in the real world, is a valuable tool for fashion and retail. This practical application allows users to try on digital fashion using a smartphone or other device and can be an aid for making purchase decisions for physical items. However, the rendering quality we see today may vary depending on the types of items.

Popular YouTuber, Safia Nygaard, conducted an AR experiment in which she aimed to test the realism of digital fashion using her three million followers on Instagram. After trying out AR clothing through a phone filter, she decided to create professional photographs, wearing digital fashion for a week, and post the images daily. She selected her outfits from DRESSX, the app-based digital fashion marketplace, with her first selection, at $30, being a black and gold dress and jacket combination.

Per the app's instructions, Nygaard had a full-body photo taken of her with minimal clothing and sent the photo to the DRESSX team with her outfit choice. After receiving her photo back, fully "dressed" in the new digital outfit, she posted the augmented reality photo to Instagram. The result? Within her usual one thousand-plus comments, it was clear that plenty of people believed it was a real dress.

Others questioned their vision, "Are my eyes glitching, or does this look a little off to anyone else?" and "It's so cool! But is this a photoshopped outfit? Am I losing it?" (Nygaard 2021)

According to experts, AR technology is still nascent and not as mature as today's virtual reality (Meige et al. 2022). But imagine how time-saving AR digital fashion could be for influencers who post outfits every day—once the digital fashion renders more realistically. AR continues to evolve and can be a great tool for certain fashion categories.

Today, one can go on Instagram, try on various sunglasses, and take a selfie in each pair to make a purchase decision. The social media app, Snapchat, owned by Snap, is by far the most advanced social media app when it comes to AR.

Snap has thousands of filters on their Dress Up tab and an AR lens that allows users to try on items like virtual sneakers from Nike or Puma, clothing from Farfetch or American Eagle, and even jewelry from Cartier. Some of their lenses even allow users to transform themselves into characters through selfie photos and videos with AI-generated filters. Snap, whose camera app is one of its biggest strengths, states, "approximately two out of every three Snapchatters engage with AR on our service daily and play with lenses over six billion times per day on average" (Snap Inc. 2023).

Using a camera filter is a common way to use augmented reality for fashion. Numerous independent brands and individual creators are designing filters with jewelry items, makeup looks, clothing, and accessories. DRESSX, which is powered by Snap, Inc. technology, has made a name for itself by not only creating its own digital dress designs for AR but also partnering with fashion brands like Jason Wu, Tommy Hilfiger, and Adidas, as well as many indie designers. Anyone can try on and take a selfie of the digital designs for free, or they can purchase 3D looks on the marketplace app for their digital closet.

As advanced as Snap has gotten in its AR capabilities, the rendering of the items varies in quality. For example, on DRESSX, I tried on an AR iridescent multicolored bucket hat and captured a selfie that looked entirely genuine. However, when I experimented with a dress and necklace, the lighting of the items differed from my surroundings, making it more challenging to achieve a realistic look. As with any technology, AR requires testing and refinement, and this is the phase it is currently in.

AR FOR FASHION AND RETAIL

During New York Fashion Week, one innovative brand—Private Policy—placed QR codes around the city that allowed the public to try on, using AR, three virtual looks from their physical runway (McDowell 2023). During my enlightened conversation with Sonya Hartmann, an accomplished technology expert and former head of the Metaverse launch for Meta, she expressed her unwavering belief that augmented reality for fashion is truly the next big thing. In the near future, stores may introduce virtual mirrors that enable shoppers to try on outfits virtually to assess what is worth taking into the fitting room and undressing for.

Zero10, a fashion AR start-up, is making strides in bringing these cutting-edge AR mirrors into physical stores. I had the opportunity to try their mirror and app, capturing numerous videos of myself wearing virtual outfits. Though they didn't look entirely lifelike, the experience proved incredibly valuable as it enabled me to swiftly try on various looks. As a result, I was able to decide which pieces I would genuinely wear as physical items, which ones I preferred solely for the virtual realm, and which ones I didn't desire at all.

AR can serve as an overlay of digital fashion on a real person, and it can also be in the form of, say, a virtual fashion show overlayed on real city streets and viewed through a device like a tablet or a phone. Mixed reality (MR) takes this concept further—with AR glasses. MR creates a multilayered reality where lines are also blurred between the digital and physical, taking in the surroundings and projecting virtual objects onto them.

For mixed reality, imagine shopping in a retail store wearing AR glasses. As you gaze at different items, relevant information seamlessly appears. The information provides details, prices, and even the option to add these items to your virtual shopping cart for home delivery. It's a transformative experience that merges the convenience of online shopping with the tangible environment of a physical store. Headsets and glasses have not gained widespread popularity, but there is a promising shift on the horizon. They will likely become more compelling to the average consumer once they: (1) evolve to seamlessly integrate AR with our surroundings, much like the newly released Apple Vision Pro, and (2) become more accessible in price and size.

VIRTUAL REALITY

Virtual reality (VR) stands at the core of the Metaverse experience. For avid gamers, VR has become commonplace, but for nongamers, VR is an entirely new experience. As discussed in earlier chapters, through VR, we delve into immersive 3D experiences, taking on the form of an avatar to explore virtual worlds in real time.

Over time, as the technology and networks have advanced, the VR quality of virtual games has significantly improved, leading us to a pivotal moment. We now stand at an inflection point where the cutting-edge 3D technology used in gaming engines like Unreal Engine and Unity will transcend gaming.

The VR realm harnesses this same game engine technology for extensive applications and a multitude of purposes. Although we have yet to achieve the full realization of the Metaverse, virtual reality is present in many places around us. Numerous real-world applications, known as "use cases," validate how useful VR can be utilized across many sectors. A noteworthy example is the Hong Kong Airport, which leverages the Unity game engine to implement a VR digital twin (Ball 2022, 106).

A digital twin refers to a digital replica of a physical entity, including systems, processes, and more. Using real-time data and simulations within the digital twin, Hong Kong Airport's leaders can test different scenarios and make informed decisions regarding security, staffing, and other crucial factors. This technology makes Hong Kong a "smart airport" (Indovance 2022).

Pilots have been learning how to fly using flight simulators for years, which is probably one of the most advanced forms of virtual reality in use today. And surgeons at Johns Hopkins University are performing live spinal surgeries using game engine rendering technology (Ball 2022, 229). An example of a more common virtual reality use case is in real estate. Three-dimensional tours of homes are helping agents sell properties at a 9 percent higher price. Staging homes using VR can save agents over $2,000 per month. And developers can use VR to sell a building that isn't even built yet (Abualzolof 2022).

The best example of virtual reality for the average person is in gaming, as discussed in previous chapters. And the community, creativity, and breadth of virtual worlds closest matching the future Metaverse are found in *Roblox*, the platform with forty million games and over sixty million average users. This highly successful platform does not require a headset, which, as noted earlier, is a device that has not been widely adopted. Meta, however, required a headset when they launched their virtual world, *Horizon Worlds*.

In my conversation with Hartmann, the former Meta executive who's been working in VR tech for several years, we discussed the reasoning behind Meta's decision to prioritize virtual reality for headset usage rather than creating a more accessible virtual world for web and mobile platforms.

She recalled that the initial strategy of releasing it in headset first was the vision to bring to life a "Ready Player One"-inspired experience—as in the movie—because "experientially, the headset is a much more intimate type of experience." Like *Roblox*, *Horizon Worlds* also enables users to become creators of experiences, but there were several initial challenges for the user.

She explained the user-creators had incredible ideas, but, unfortunately, the technology and networks could not catch up to the consumer appetite. The system had bugginess issues, and without sensors to recognize leg movements, the avatars were initially legless.

Another challenge is Meta's avatars, which are only useable on their own platforms. When it comes to avatars for the Metaverse, Hartmann predicts an avatar platform that is open and interoperable—can work across many platforms—like Ready Player Me, may win out because "people will not want to create themselves for ten different locations."

Virtual reality has been successful even without the use of headsets—from virtual gaming platforms like *Fortnite*, *Minecraft*, and *Roblox* to real estate, surgeries, and industrial digital twins. Virtual reality is also utilized by some brands, who are experimenting with VR experiences to connect with their customers, sometimes linked directly from their websites.

VR FOR FASHION AND RETAIL

When I entered Dior Beauty's Miss Dior's virtual world as an avatar they provided, it was mesmerizing. I was transported to France for a summer day in Provence at the majestic Chateau de La Colle Noire, a replica of the building where Christian Dior had his office (Intravaia 2021). I walked through the expansive entry garden, up to the front door, and into the elegant office with a panoramic view of the beautiful countryside. Admiring the view, I proceeded through the window to vast acres of pink and coral roses. The experience kept me engaged longer than I ever would scrolling through squares on a website. In fact, in another Dior virtual world, where they collaborated with Harrod's, the average engagement time was over fifteen minutes, resulting in 18.2 percent "shop now" clicks (Emperia 2022).

As I highlighted earlier, some fashion and beauty brands have built mini virtual worlds within gaming worlds to attract large, young audiences. Others, like H&M and Dior Beauty, have created fantastical immersive virtual reality experiences to engage their own customers linked from their websites. And still, others have experimented, as part of events like Digital Fashion Week, on metaverse platforms like *Decentraland* or *The Sandbox* to learn what's possible in virtual worlds, even if the users there are limited in numbers.

I sat down with Kadine James, an accomplished creative technologist who was in town from London. James has produced fantastical metaverse experiences with Yahoo, Artificial Rome, and Immersive Kind, as well as AR filters on Instagram—including a bejeweled gold crown, which I tried on, to commemorate Queen Elizabeth's Jubilee. James emphasized the critical need for fashion brands to embrace these cutting-edge technologies to remain relevant to the upcoming generations. She highlighted the "mind-blowing" ABBA Voyage show as a compelling example of virtual experiences' immense power to unite people and captivate their imagination.

While some brands are creating temporary virtual reality experiences, others are buying more permanent virtual land. It remains to be seen how people will want to explore and shop in the Metaverse. Virtual platforms like *Decentraland* or *The Sandbox* are land-based finite spaces with plots of land. Within these platform's apps, users can enter the virtual spaces in different ways. They can walk around and explore, or they can directly enter a space by clicking on a box on the home page, the way Netflix displays shows and movies, or they can type the coordinates—like a street address—to get to an exact location.

This consumer preference for how to navigate a metaverse experience and whether land makes sense is still an unknown aspect of this future internet. In the meantime, some companies are buying virtual real estate to build virtual shopping centers. Gucci owns land in *The Sandbox*, and Adidas owns land in both *Decentraland* and *The Sandbox*. Republic Realm paid $4.2 million for space in *The Sandbox* and opened a shopping district in *Decentraland* called Metajuku. Although digital fashion brands like DRESSX and Tribute have signed leases there, physical fashion brands have not done so, but this could be because of timing, as we are still in the early days (Bain 2022).

Fashion and beauty brands are utilizing virtual reality to create captivating and immersive experiences for their customers. These virtual worlds transport users to stunning locations, fostering deep engagement and, at times, resulting in increased conversion rates. Other brands have targeted younger audiences through gaming platforms. These experiences are often temporary; therefore, some companies are purchasing virtual real estate to establish future shopping destinations. Although certain aspects of the Metaverse remain uncertain, like the importance of owning land, the evolving nature of VR is bound to create immersive experiences that will naturally draw consumers in.

If the ABBA Voyage show has taught us anything, it's that people desire transformative experiences that evoke powerful emotions, even if they exist beyond the boundaries of traditional reality. Augmented and mixed realities currently offer enjoyment and convenience on an individual level, but it is virtual reality that has the potential to transport individuals, *as well as groups*, into extraordinary encounters that leave a lasting impact on their hearts and minds.

Virtual reality is the essence of the Metaverse and Web 3.0. In the next chapter, we will delve into another important technological aspect of Web 3.0, namely the blockchain. In fact, blockchain technologies are often referred to as Web3, a slight variation in spelling. And within the realm of the blockchain, we can gain insight into the various uses of the collectible digital assets known as NFTs.

CHAPTER 6

NFTS AND THE BLOCKCHAIN

We've been sold on this concept of direct-to-consumer, which ultimately is not all that direct.

—TY HANEY, FOUNDER, OUTDOOR VOICES AND TYB

On a hot summer weekend in 2021, following a delightful dinner with friends, I found myself swaying to the music on the open-air dance floor of Calissa, a restaurant in Water Mill, New York, known for its summer concerts. I was absorbed by the captivating beats spun by a favorite DJ/producer, my hairline damp, and my energy elevated.

As the final notes of the night reverberated, I was a little star stuck when RAC, the DJ, and I made eye contact. Elated, I bounded onto the small platform to chat and seize the chance to capture a picture with one of my music idols. Later, as I prepared to tag him in my Instagram story, I curiously went into his profile and stumbled upon a series of video artworks called NFTs, featuring his music. Intrigued by their cutting-edge beauty, I embarked on a quest to understand the world of NFTs. I discovered that through them, I could own a unique piece of this producer's musical artistry. It also led me down the rabbit hole of cryptocurrency, the blockchain, and ultimately the realm of the Metaverse.

A DIGITAL ARTIST'S DREAM

NFTs weren't just *my* first introduction to Web 3.0. Six months before I had ever heard of them, Laurie Segall, whom I interviewed for this book, was making her first discovery. Segall, a former technology correspondent for CNN, created the start-up beat at the network when companies like Instagram and Uber were launching. After convincing the executives in the corner office that, yes, people would get into strangers' cars, and they would stay in strangers' homes, via apps like Uber and Airbnb, she went on to interview every major tech titan, including Meta CEO Mark Zuckerberg, Apple CEO Tim Cook, and tech entrepreneur Sam Altman, who became OpenAI CEO.

Segall, who tells scintillating stories of the tech world in her book, *Special Characters: My Adventures with Tech's Titans and Misfits,* is one who has a pulse on what people will want in the future.

When the most expensive NFT ever sold made headlines in 2021, Segall, feeling a familiar wave of energy, "knew that this moment in time represented something much larger." So she spent a week profiling, for *60 Minutes,* the pioneering digital artist who created it.

Mike Winkelmann, who goes by Beeple, was a freelance graphic artist whose work included projects for Nike and Apple and digital visuals at concerts for artists like Justin Bieber and Katy Perry. He looks more "computer nerd" than artist. In 2007, he started producing 3D digital artwork for himself on his computer as a daily hobby. He got into the habit of making new artwork based on current events, every day after work, some of them being quite bizarre. He was never able to monetize his personal artwork until, finally, NFTs gave him that ability, and he sold a few.

After thirteen years of producing the "Everydays," as Beeple calls them, he had amassed five thousand of them. Working with a partner, he put together a collage of the first five thousand to be sold at auction as one massive NFT (SXSW 2022). On March 11, 2021, Christie's announced on Twitter that Beeple's NFT made history. "*The First 5000 Days*, the first purely digital NFT-based artwork offered by a major auction house, has sold for $69 million, positioning him among the top three most valuable living artists" (Christie's 2021).

The Beeple event changed history by bringing the first NFT into an auction house well-known for fine art and collectibles. But, even more importantly, art in digital form, which used to be easily copied and pasted, could finally claim a value the way other art does.

Why is it such a big deal for digital artists, whether graphic or music, to turn their work into NFTs, and why only now? Laurie Segall was right when she said NFTs represented something larger. What makes this all possible is the blockchain, which together with cloud and edge computing, has the potential to revolutionize the tech industry (Dey 2023).

ON-CHAIN MAKES IT ALL POSSIBLE
The word blockchain, to me, evokes an image of two hard objects and is harsh and intimidating. It took me quite a while to understand it, and I am certainly no expert, but I will offer a simplified explanation that will help us apply it for our purposes. The blockchain allows for more direct transactions. The Metaverse needs to be interoperable; our avatars need to seamlessly navigate and transact between many virtual worlds. The two will be more easily integrated if the Metaverse is "on-chain" or on the blockchain, though no one can say if it actually will be.

The blockchain cuts out the middleman, such as banks for consumers, data-collecting social apps for brands, or streaming services for musical artists. In essence, the blockchain provides a more direct way to perform verified and transparent transactions between two parties.

On the blockchain, I can trade currency without a bank, and an artist can sell art or music directly to a fan. That currency is in the form of a cryptocurrency token, which is fungible—a unit can be traded for another of the same—and the art is "minted" in the form of a non-fungible token, or NFT. You need crypto to buy an NFT of art, music, and so on, but an NFT is an asset, not a currency.

The blockchain, which is digital, gets its name because the transactions are permanently recorded in blocks of numbers, forming a chain of those blocks of numbers. When I make a transaction with my regular bank, there is a transaction number recorded with a long string of digits. If I create and sell something on the *blockchain*, there is also a transaction number for that sale, and it is recorded on a digital ledger.

The person who bought it has a unique wallet with a unique number that can be associated with that person. If that person then sells the item to someone else, my original transaction number is, forever, the first string of numbers—as a block—on that ledger, and the new transaction becomes a second string, or block, of numbers, recorded on the ledger. So, that item's history is now a chain of two transactions that are linked or chained together. As it continues to change hands, the chain grows with more blocks of numbers as a permanent record.

How does this benefit artists and creators? The creator will get a royalty every time the work changes hands because the first block of numbers represents the creator, and a royalty amount will be attached to the item, say 10 percent, that goes to that creator. For example, Beeple sold an earlier artwork as an NFT for $67,000 in crypto. When he became more well-known, and that owner sold it to someone else, Beeple earned another $660,000, which was 10 percent of that sale (Mapperson 2021).

If the art had been a regular painting without an NFT associated with it, he would not have earned anything in the second sale. The same applies to musicians who sell music on the blockchain. In RAC's case, he created music in collaboration with digital art, another imaginative way to create an NFT.

How does the blockchain benefit brands? A brand's creation can be minted as an NFT, and it can benefit the brand as any digital art does. The digital asset can be digital clothing, a digital bag, or any other digital item. But brands that have been experimenting with NFTs have had success with NFTs that provide additional benefits to the owner. "Membership" NFTs, especially those combined with physical items, build loyalty and foster deeper communities.

MEMBERSHIP NFTS

In 2021 and 2022, some "breaking news" events were happening in the world of NFTs that captured the attention of celebrity types and luxury brands. One was Beeple, and another was the Bored Ape Yacht Club (BAYC). The domino effect of these events seemed to correlate with the timing of luxury brands entering Web 3.0—beginning with NFTs and soon after entering virtual worlds through gaming.

The idea for the Bored Ape Yacht Club began on Twitter, the social media favorite of early adopters of cryptocurrency. With the pandemic causing a lot of boredom, two crypto-loving friends wanted to hang out with like-minded others who liked to go "all in," a.k.a. "aping" into something risky like crypto. They came up with an idea to combine digital art and the crypto community. So they got two techy friends to help them. They created ten thousand NFTs, each with its own unique cartoon portrait of an ape, basically a jpeg that comes with a "membership" and perks for their holders.

One perk included a party for "club" members on a real yacht in New York. Each BAYC NFT was originally priced at 0.08 Ethereum (ETH), a cryptocurrency, that was about $300 at the time (Hissong 2021). As of the writing of this book, the lowest priced BAYC NFTs sell on OpenSea, an NFT marketplace, for about 46 ETH, or $83,000. Because an NFT sale always provides a royalty to the original creator, the BAYC founders continue to make money in the resale market. This economic advantage is one reason Web 3.0 is considered a "creator's economy."

Many people followed the hype and dramatic impact made by NFTs in the worlds of art, music, sports, luxury, and fashion. Some tech-savvy consumers rushed to marketplaces like Nifty Gateway and OpenSea to buy them and then witnessed the speed with which the values of these digital assets plunged. But this volatility is par for the course at the beginning of a new era. For the purpose of this book, I have focused on art and luxury because it deeply relates to fashion. I delve into why NFTs are not going away and, in fact, make a lot of sense for certain sectors.

NFTS AND THE LUXURY MARKET

The luxury fashion market has entered the NFT space, and the stories of BAYC and Beeple represent the two types of NFTs that make sense for many industries, Digital Collectibles, and Digital Collectibles with Membership. In both cases, there is a version that makes even more sense for fashion—an NFT that includes a physical twin. RTFKT, a start-up pronounced "artifact," whose sneakerhead founders produced sneaker NFTs, was acquired by Nike. Now, many of their NFT drops include both a physical twin, as well as membership perks.

According to *Forbes*, "NFTs make it possible for luxury brands to create priceless, irreplicable experiences for customers which will, in turn, improve brand awareness, engagement, and boost sales" (DeAcetis 2021). NFTs have been a part of fashion weeks for multiple seasons already. Luxury brands were some of the early adopters of NFT releases from 2022, and they were usually done in collaboration with digital expert partnerships.

Dolce & Gabbana was the first to release an NFT collection of nine pieces, of which five of them came with custom physical pieces. The collection sold out for $6 million. Gucci offered one-of-a-kind sneakers as NFTs (DeAcetis 2021). Moncler offered NFTs related to their platinum-colored jacket. Tag Heuer debuted a smartwatch that allows users to display their NFTs on the watch's face as their digital identity (Sinclair 2023).

It makes sense that NFTs are particularly appealing to luxury consumers. Many luxury items are already collectible, and NFTs allow brands to offer special privileges. Tiffany made NFTs available to "members only" of CryptoPunks—one of the original exclusive membership NFT collections—that were tied to physical jewelry—a pendant of the CryptoPunk. They retailed for $50,000 each, and all 250 of them sold out (Akhtar 2022). Morgan Stanley believes the Metaverse, gaming, and NFT sectors could represent 10 percent of the luxury goods market by 2030 (Canny 2023), so it makes sense that Gucci formed a permanent team dedicated to the Metaverse (Ryder 2022).

IT'S COMPLICATED

NFTs are not just for expensive art and luxury collectibles. Nike created an NFT marketplace called Dot Swoosh, or .Swoosh, that allows users to collect, display, create, and trade their NFTs.

As research for this book, I set out to buy a phygital NFT from Nike's RTFKT collection, including both a digital asset and a physical twin sneaker. I was intrigued by the NFT collection designed by Takashi Murakami for RTFKT x Nike Airforce 1, labeled SZN1. I chose to purchase one of the ten different styles offered, a graphite gray and purple virtual sneaker NFT, which gave me access to order the complimentary physical sneakers in my size, albeit without ever seeing them in physical form.

I will have to wait about six months to receive the physical pair because it is made to order, and, as is typical for transacting on the blockchain, the process to order them was not simple.

Luckily, I already had a crypto wallet. Step one was to buy the first "unboxing" NFT to "forge" it, and step two was to use the "forged" NFT to order the physical sneaker in the correct size. I imported my crypto wallet, moved the cryptocurrency into the wallet, and bought the preforged NFT. Then things got a little tricky.

I needed a little help, so I joined their Discord community to learn how to "forge" the NFT by the deadline. There, I connected with very friendly RTFKT NFT owners, as well as a company representative, who went out of their way to help me. I now own the forged NFT, have a membership in the community with access to early drops and in-person events, and have a physical pair of sneakers on order. These are great benefits for loyal customers, but the process wasn't simple. This on-chain complexity has led some brands to simplify things behind the scenes, relegating the tech to the backend.

Some fashion brands recognize the value of NFTs for their business, but they have seen that for many customers, the process of buying one can be a major obstacle, especially if a physical item has to be ordered in a certain size.

WHAT'S IN A NAME?
I spent much more time buying the RTFKT NFT than I would for an ordinary item online; however, the pride of ownership and belonging made it seem worthwhile. Alo Yoga is one of the brands that has figured out how to provide the same benefits of community building without the obstacles of transacting on chain. They launched a premium collection of their apparel, paired with NFTs that came

with perks but decided to forgo the NFT-based language to make it a seamless experience.

When the Alo customers purchased an item from the premium physical collection, they were also given a 3D digital twin (NFT), which unlocked rewards such as access to their wellness clubs throughout the world, a private client manager, and access to exclusive items.

Alo's crypto payment process was handled on the backend so whether the customer was buying the premium collection because they loved the clothing, or whether they were buying it because they wanted the NFT, there was no difference. They did not need to have a crypto wallet, nor need to know what NFTs were. Their purchase gave them an engaging digital experience in addition to the physical, premium product. (Schulz 2023). Brands are recognizing that it pays to simplify when it comes to NFTs.

DECENTRALIZATION
There is a reason that brands continue to experiment with NFTs, and building loyalty is one of the most compelling. It is challenging for brands to connect directly with customers in a centralized system with a middleman, like a social media corporation or a bank, exercising control over the transactions and data. Ty Haney, the founder of Outdoor Voices, notes that the brand would "spend 30 percent to 40 percent of their dollars raised directly to the big [social media] platforms." Yet, managing customer relationships across all the channels "made the strength of the community difficult to measure and made customer feedback challenging to collect" (Ramaswamy et al. 2022).

She launched a new start-up, TYB (Try Your Best), that "leverages the blockchain to allow brands to directly incentivize their fans for their loyalty and valuable actions." A decentralized system using blockchain technology makes this possible.

Imagine a world where I can buy a brand's products from several different places, and the brand can see that data and incentivize me for my loyalty. Blockchains are *decentralized*, guaranteeing transparency by making all the transaction details publicly accessible. Rather than having a center of power like a bank, they utilize sophisticated technology to validate the transactions, relying instead on a network of participants, algorithms, and data miners to do that.

Still, this complexity can be challenging for the consumer because it adds steps to the process, which slows things down, as it did for my RTFKT purchase. It also adds transaction costs called gas fees, which go to the data miners. Brands like Alo are getting around this, but ultimately it requires some education on the consumer side.

Decentralization is widely regarded as the future, and blockchain technology plays a crucial role in enabling it through the use of tokens, such as cryptocurrencies or NFTs. The evolution of NFTs has expanded their scope beyond purely representing digital assets. They now encompass memberships and even more groundbreaking phygital NFTs that combine physical assets with digital ownership. This is a huge unlock for brands.

NFTs provide creators and brands with unparalleled advantages like fostering a sense of community and loyalty that surpasses any previous means of engagement. These benefits enable a more exclusive and direct relationship between creators, brands, and their audiences.

Although decentralized platforms currently present obstacles for end users, brands, and tech start-ups like TYB are actively working to address these pain points. It's important to understand the blockchain because it's possible the next era of the internet will use this technology. For now, we will continue to focus on the many benefits of virtual worlds, which currently exist both on and off the blockchain.

PART III

A PEOPLE PERSPECTIVE

CHAPTER 7

BENEFITS FOR CONSUMERS

I don't think that (the Metaverse) is primarily about being engaged with the internet more. I think it's about being engaged more naturally.
—MARK ZUCKERBERG, CEO, META

Choosing to wear a Chanel look for the first time in her life, Hetty Mahlich describes her experience.

I go for a long white column dress with a black dropped-waist band—an iconic Chanel avant-garde silhouette—featuring the house's camelia flower motif, first introduced in the 1920s. Simple, yet elegant, it's intrinsically Chanel… As a brand well out of my and most other normal folks' budget, wearing Chanel, albeit in digital form, is an experience in itself. When I look down, I can see the dress ripple as I twirl my hips. Around me, I see my companions dressed up and transformed. We all look noticeably more elegant than we do in reality. One woman remarks that she never wears high heels, "isn't this exciting!" (Mahlich 2022)

Hetty vividly recalls her memorable entrance into the enchanting world of Bal de Paris, a virtual reality experience hosted by Chanel in May 2022. With a headset on, she and others immersed themselves in a fantastical music and dance performance. Hetty twirled and danced in her elegant Chanel dress, cherishing every moment of the social and unforgettable evening.

ENGAGEMENT AND ENTERTAINMENT

While the Chanel experience was an in-person event requiring a headset, it's a great example of how consumers are enjoying the benefits of virtual reality. It can be social and fun, allowing us to wear things we couldn't otherwise, like the Chanel dress and high heels. In recent years, a wave of *online* virtual experiences have also allowed customers to engage with brands in entertaining new ways.

In 2023, H&M introduced a more interactive virtual experience on *Roblox,* which, like other gaming platforms, is not on the blockchain. Visitors had fun with fabrics in different colors, materials, and textures to create over one thousand different in-game digital garments (Edelson 2023).

Polo Ralph Lauren created a ski shop in the same platform, surrounded by snowy mountain peaks, and stocked it with virtual puffer jackets, beanies, and skiwear that players could buy for their avatars for under $5 each (Debter 2022). Brands such as Tommy Hilfiger, Nike, and Gucci engaged with new customers through *Roblox* "worlds" as well, while still other brands partnered with the games of *Fortnite* or *The Sandbox* (Bein 2023; Owusu 2022; Anyanwu 2021).

Some brands, including Burberry, Lacoste, and Uniqlo, partnered with *Minecraft*, one of the most successful games in the world. In the Burberry experience, players, for example, could see Burberry's Equestrian Knight character come to life, making a deep connection with the heritage brand.

Burberry also created a physical capsule collection based on the game and displayed screens of the game in seven of their global store locations. A Burberry executive shared his thoughts. "Gaming is a super important channel for us in terms of how we engage our customers. We know it's a very important passion point for our target markets and consumers. We know they are there, they are present, and they're very active in that community." It's not Burberry's first gaming experience, and it likely won't be their last (Schulz 2022).

Similarly, Lacoste's *Minecraft* world featured a giant crocodile, a tennis court, and a beach, inspiring the creation of a capsule collection of both physical and digital items, including apparel, accessories, and footwear adorned with both the Lacoste and *Minecraft* pixelated logos (Lacoste 2022). In 2020, Uniqlo kept it simple by offering free in-game T-shirts while producing corresponding physical ones for their stores, allowing players to dress the same in real life (Adams 2020). The following year, Uniqlo expanded its *Minecraft* partnership, introducing a more extensive collection with physical and digital T-shirts, hoodies, and bags (Jones, 2021).

Beyond gaming platforms, another compelling example of user engagement through immersive technologies comes in the form of stand-alone gaming apps. Louis Vuitton, to celebrate the two-hundredth anniversary of the founder's birthday, launched an entertaining video game called *Louis the Game* on the Apple App Store. Players took the shape of a branded avatar, progressing through levels, collecting artistic postcards—some of them designed by Beeple—and ultimately arriving at the big birthday bash (Lloyd-Smith 2021).

A year later, Louis Vuitton released another gaming experience on the Apple App Store, this time incorporating augmented reality. In 2023, LVMH, the parent company of Louis Vuitton, partnered directly with Epic Games, the creator of *Fortnite* and Unreal Engine, to develop immersive experiences for their suite of brands, including Dior, Celine, and Bulgari. An executive from the brand expressed their enthusiasm that this partnership will accelerate their expertise in 3D tools and ecosystems and help them engage more effectively with young generations (Kelly 2023).

This convergence of fashion and gaming is revolutionizing the way brands connect with their audience, creating immersive experiences that blur the boundaries between virtual and physical realms. However, it's not just brands that are embracing the Metaverse. Retailers like Bloomingdales and Selfridges have also delved into this new frontier.

Arriving at Selfridges virtual store in *Decentraland*, a metaverse platform on the blockchain, one was greeted by a doorman at a building that resembled the Selfridges in Birmingham, England. They claimed to be the "first to launch a department store in the Metaverse" (Hooi 2022). Similarly, Bloomingdale's experimented with a virtual store that showcased brands like Marc Jacobs, Ralph Lauren, and David Yurman. Later, they launched a holiday-themed virtual store with various brand spaces and immersive rooms (Walk-Morris 2022).

As brands with sufficient budgets explore the possibilities of Web 3.0 and the Metaverse, they utilize different approaches. These early adopter endeavors offer valuable insights. At this early stage of a new era, these experimental creations provide two huge benefits. First, these brands are learning many new and creative ways to engage with their customers. Second, it provides a learning opportunity for other brands observing from these use cases. As the fashion industry collectively learns from the early adopters, more brands can join in as best practices become established.

Louis Vuitton, for example, evolved their app concept by incorporating an augmented reality factor in the second release. The ideas keep evolving, and the most successful ones will endure. One thing remains clear: these brands are relentlessly pushing forward, continuously testing, learning, and evolving with metaverse experiences.

For many of these brands, customer engagement has been the initial entry point to understanding the Metaverse and all it has to offer. It provides entertainment for the user and allows brands to connect with their super fans and gain new fans in ways previously unimaginable.

COMMUNITY AND SOCIALIZATION

Customer engagement may be the initial reason for brands to experiment with virtual worlds. It's true that centralized gaming platforms, like *Roblox, Fortnite*, and *Minecraft*, currently boast a larger user base compared to decentralized virtual worlds on the blockchain, such as *Decentraland* and *The Sandbox*. However, the landscape is evolving, and as time goes on, decentralized platforms will likely become a game changer. As demonstrated earlier, whether playing games or engaging with brands, the top reason why many gamers go into the gaming platform is because of the community. We've already seen how virtual gaming worlds are the social networks of Gen Z.

As these virtual worlds continue to flourish, people will continue to find their tribes there. And by using avatars, they will achieve a stronger sense of connection than mere messaging. Reflecting on my personal experience with the online forum during my medical situation, I recall that while messaging provided privacy, it felt somewhat detached. However, if I envision the same scenario, instead as an immersive virtual world with avatars, I am confident it would feel more natural and comforting—and less self-conscious than video platforms like Zoom. Virtual worlds are compelling because of the sense of belonging and community they foster, which makes them ideal spaces for people to form meaningful connections and support one another.

Gamers seem to have figured out the benefits of connecting in virtual worlds. According to one extensive report about gaming in the

US, 83 percent of gamers play with others online or in-person versus alone (Entertainment Software Association 2022). In another survey, 83 percent of responding gamers in the US stated that video games had "introduced them to new friendships and relationships, and 46 percent of respondents stated that they had met a good friend, spouse, or significant other through gaming" (Clement 2022).

These numbers would not be surprising to the makers of the top gaming consoles, PlayStation and Xbox, who designed them with socialization in mind. As early as 2008, Microsoft and Sony were pushing for these gaming consoles to be a "place to go to play, communicate, and socialize with buddies, melding the virtual world with the real one" (Taub 2008). They recognized then that a virtual/gaming world was about much more than playing a game. Fifteen years later, the stats above prove they were right.

For some adults, even major life events are happening in virtual worlds. Traci and Dave Gagnon "got married in the Metaverse on a Labor Day weekend." It was a hybrid event; the live wedding was held at a country club in New Hampshire, where they live, and the virtual wedding was held in Virbela, a company that builds virtual environments for events. Guests who couldn't attend in person attended via a computer.

The idea made sense to the couple because they met as avatars in 2015 at a virtual company event in Las Vegas. In speaking about the wedding, Ms. Gagnon reflected, "the experience of moving through a virtual world as an avatar creates a more immersive, emotionally satisfying experience than Zoom" (Kurutz 2021). Family events in the Metaverse are not commonplace yet, but if they were, we could imagine having to dress our avatars for these occasions.

Lincoln Donelan runs parties for partygoers in his hometown of Melbourne, Australia, as well as virtually for avatars on the platform *VRChat*. During the pandemic lockdown, *VRChat's* number of daily users steadily increased and even now has surpassed prepandemic levels. Outside a virtual club called Tube, the streets look a lot like East London, with retail shops on the canal, and people's avatars show up as anime, animals, or other fantastical characters they've created. *VRChat* has hundreds of thousands of virtual worlds people have created to socialize in avatar form.

One user, Turels, a former musician with a medical condition that prevented him from performing, became a virtual DJ after being encouraged by friends he made at the virtual club. He now performs regularly there (Faber 2022).

Meta may not have gotten it right the first time with *Horizon Worlds*, but CEO Mark Zuckerberg recognizes that a 3D experience is the next evolution of social engagement. He told his employees his future vision of Facebook is not the two-dimensional version we're using today, but instead, it is in the Metaverse. He described the Metaverse as "an embodied internet… a persistent, synchronous environment where we can be together." He believes it will resemble "a hybrid between the social platforms that we see today (and) an environment where you're embodied in it" (Newton 2021). Perhaps, without the need for a headset and with avatars that feel less "cartoony," it will achieve the mass adoption he predicts.

People are engaging and connecting in virtual worlds in many ways already. For those who are not, we can imagine that it may, in fact, be "more natural" to shop in a virtual world than it is in the dot com world. After all, shopping in physical stores has often been a social thing.

Malls are not as popular as they once were, but they still get groups together for movies, eating, and some shopping. Stores' fitting rooms often have friends or couples trying on for each other. This is something that is missing from online shopping, but if we consider the examples above, with the various activities happening in virtual worlds like *VRChat,* shopping as a social activity starts to make sense again.

SUSTAINABILITY
As much as clothing is the ultimate form of self-expression, not many people can afford a new outfit for every occasion. Nor is that sustainable. Fashion accounts for 10 percent of the world's carbon emissions and is the second-most polluting industry in the world (Donald 2022). Even fashion influencers have to get creative with how they can show a new outfit every day to keep the attention of their followers. Whether it's an influencer or the average person posting on social media, the prevalence of images and selfies creates an unprecedented demand for nonrepeating outfits.

One alternative that emerged to fill this need has been fashion rental services. Rent the Runway began as a place to rent eveningwear for special occasions. However, demand grew so much that by 2016, they began a subscription service, which allowed users to rent multiple items and types of clothing on a monthly basis. The worldwide apparel rental market in 2022 was projected at $5.9 billion, and the expectation is that it will grow to $7.5 billion by 2026 (Smith 2022).

Another alternative to buying clothes is buying pre-owned clothing in marketplaces like thredUP, Poshmark, and The RealReal. There is no longer a stigma to wearing preworn clothing. In fact, these now-established start-ups are marketing themselves as sustainably focused fashion alternatives because today's younger generations would rather spend less on their wardrobes and save the planet in the process. They are also living their lives on their phones. In 2022, teenagers spent almost half of their waking hours on mobile devices versus 24 percent in 2015 (Vogels 2022). And with more and more of them becoming content creators, there is a bigger need to have more outfit changes.

A pair of Ukrainian-born entrepreneurs, Daria Shapovalova and Natalia Modenova, found inspiration through a Barclay study showing that 9 percent of fashion purchases in the UK were solely for the purpose of content creation and were returned after use. In 2019, they launched an agency with pop-up stores in Los Angeles specifically for content creators, providing clothing and video production for a rental fee. Then the pandemic hit, and they moved their business online, soon realizing that you could fill the void more sustainably: digital fashion. They launched a new business model, naming it DRESSX, as the first and largest digital-only fashion brand in 2020 (DELL 2021).

Just like rental and pre-owned fashion, digital fashion is an alternative to purchasing new physical goods. As more events move to the Metaverse, sustainability will be an added benefit to moving in that direction. Customers who spend more time in virtual reality will likely consume less physical clothing over time, perhaps leading to a shift in production by the fashion industry. Based on the success of alternative forms of fashion, it is evident that sustainability is important to many consumers and another benefit of a digital identity.

It's also important to note that we do not yet know the sustainability implications of the Metaverse, especially if it ends up being on the blockchain. The blockchain has had major issues with energy usage, especially from cryptocurrencies like Bitcoin. On the other hand, there have been initiatives in place to adjust how these blockchains work, and a lot of progress has been made in cutting back on energy usage.

In the ever-evolving landscape of brands in virtual worlds, consumers enter for reasons beyond the freedom of self-expression, such as entertainment, community, and sustainability. Brands have been captivating consumers' attention in entertaining ways. Community building is a key benefit for young gamers; however, adults have also been finding their tribes in various virtual worlds, at times even meeting their future spouses. Still, another benefit for consumers is the potential positive effect on sustainability.

Although these brand experiences are still experimental, the combination of entertainment, engagement, community, and sustainability starts to open up compelling reasons to keep consumers coming back for more. In the next chapter, we'll hit on yet another benefit of the Metaverse that appeals to a specific but important group. This will include people who are looking to unleash their creativity in ways they never imagined they could.

CHAPTER 8

A CREATOR'S PARADISE

We're going to see this wild intersection of creativity and technology that will actually disrupt design in the way we saw the last ten years of content being disrupted.

—ALICE DELAHUNT, FORMER CHIEF DIGITAL & CONTENT OFFICER,
RALPH LAUREN; FOUNDER, SYKY

On February 2023, the artist Bad Bunny opened the Grammy stage singing, in Spanish, a mash-up of his hits, surrounded by colorfully clad dancers who got the audience dancing on their feet. As viewers watched on television, the closed captions appeared "[SPEAKING NON-ENGLISH; SINGING IN NON-ENGLISH]."

His album, *Un Verano Sin Ti*, or *A Summer Without You*, nominated for album of the year, was the first nomination of a Spanish-language album for the top prize. But no one thought to translate the lyrics. The memes went viral, and the CEO of the network made a permanent change, assuring that all future performances would be translated appropriately (Bonilla 2023). The viewers controlled the fate of how foreign language songs would be handled by a major network.

Consumers, not networks or brands, have the power. After all, Bad Bunny, whose name is Benito, had been Spotify's most-streamed artist for three years in a row—a direct result of the listeners. One reporter said it best, "Benito's recognition at the Grammys... is not a result of his entrance into the mainstream but rather of the mainstream being forced to reckon with the purchasing power of his legion of fans" (Bonilla 2023).

DIGITAL FASHION DESIGNERS

In today's world, creators with exceptional talent can finally be seen and heard without the control of a middleman. We see this in music and in all kinds of content creation on social media. But music, in particular, and fashion share a common thread when it comes to creation.

Similar to pop-music musicians, there are also mass-appeal fashion designers. And like indie singers/songwriters, there are also indie fashion designers. In both cases, the designer or musician is a unique creator producing artistic products that are designed to hopefully be enjoyed by large numbers of people. In today's world of likes and clicks, musicians can finally be discovered on their own merit, chosen by the people who love their work. Fashion designers have not had a similar platform to easily gain recognition for their talents.

One big difference between creators of music and fashion is the investment required. When Justin Bieber's mom put up his very first music videos on YouTube, all she needed was his voice and a camera. A fashion designer has to invest in materials and produce costly samples to bring their creations to life. Digital fashion for a virtual world changes all that.

Could it be that the Metaverse will be for aspiring fashion designers, what YouTube and Spotify have been for unknown musicians? It's already happening in gaming. In a previous chapter, we saw how RTFKT made a name for themselves with virtual sneakers and NFTs, and then they were quickly acquired by Nike. And these are the very early years.

Digital creations, as NFTs, continue to earn money for an artist even after they're sold, and fashion NFTs can be one way to monetize designs. But a digital fashion designer does not need to create NFTs to get noticed for their work in digital fashion. Just like a musician puts music up on YouTube, a digital fashion designer can create designs that go directly into a virtual platform that is not on the blockchain. Digital fashion puts the focus completely on the design without the expense and time needed to create physical samples, hire a model and photographer, and try to sell them to a retailer or build a direct-to-consumer website.

Web 3.0 does potentially create a lot of new competition for existing fashion brands because the lower investment requirements to create collections will mean many more designers can create digital versus physical fashion. And consumers will seek digital fashion in the virtual realm to dress their avatars and fill their digital closets.

It is logical to think some people can fall in love with a certain collection from a digital designer and want to own it in real life. This creates opportunities for creators and wannabe designers to test out their talent without the typical barriers to entry into the fashion industry. Even the lawyer or schoolteacher who always felt a creative urge but chose another path can learn 3D digital design and soon have a clothing collection for sale in the Metaverse.

Digital fashion that gains a following has the potential to generate demand for physical counterparts. For aspiring designers, this could be the launchpad of a new business. Established fashion brands, on the other hand, can utilize digital fashion as a way to test new styles before committing them to physical production. Whether it pertains to emerging or established designers, the immersive internet era promises an exponential amount of opportunities to experiment and innovate with design.

Of course, with the proliferation of any art form, only certain stars rise to the top. And for the average shopper, there may be a lot of weeds to sift through to find the gems. This will likely create a need for curated boutiques or fashion galleries, which is another creative opportunity for talented curators. With our imaginations, we can see that the 3D internet starts to emulate real life much more so than the scrolling style of our current 2D internet.

Gaming is already allowing creators like Mishi McDuff, founder of House of Blueberry, to show their talent in digital fashion design. Newer platforms, including The Fabricant, DRESSX, and The Dematerialized, are large marketplaces that cater specifically to 3D digital fashion. Thanks to their work, new platforms will likely continue to pop up.

A visionary former executive from the fashion industry sees the vast potential for curated marketplaces that showcase new digital creator talent. Alice Delahunt, known for her previous roles as a digital and marketing executive at Burberry and Ralph Lauren, left the corporate world to build a new fashion venture in the Web3 realm. She describes her brainchild, SYKY (pronounced *psyche*), as an "incubator, marketplace, and social community for the next generation of fashion designers and consumers." In a compelling interview with *TechCrunch* in January 2023, Delahunt expressed her belief "that the luxury fashion houses of tomorrow are being built today" (Hall 2023).

NEW CONTENT CREATORS

When gamers discovered the digital fashion created by Mishi McDuff, it was because she was dressing her avatar in her own designs. Not only can new digital designers *create* in the 3D internet era, but they can also promote their own work or even become virtual influencers. In fact, it's likely that many more people will become content creators or virtual influencers than there are currently on social media platforms.

For those who would like to share content but are too self-conscious to post live videos, the Metaverse is a great option because there's no need to be in front of a camera or have a certain appearance. This is game-changing. There is potentially a whole pool of talent that could be great stylists but are camera-shy. Now they will have their chance.

Young Americans, in particular, are very interested in becoming influencers (Jennings 2022). A survey conducted with two thousand interviews by Morning Consult found that 54 percent of Americans aged thirteen to thirty-eight would become an influencer if given the chance. Another study by Harris Poll of three thousand kids in both the US and the UK found that given the choice of becoming a teacher, a professional athlete, a musician, an astronaut, or a YouTuber, nearly 30 percent ranked YouTuber as their top choice (Morning Consult n.d.).

Social media has shown us that influencers don't need to be in a human form to be successful. Computer-generated or animated virtual fashion influencers have gained huge followers on platforms like Instagram. Miquela Sousa, a.k.a. Lil Miquela, an AI robot that resembles a human, "lives" in Los Angeles and has close to three million Instagram followers. She has worked with brands like Chanel, Prada, and many others. Balenciaga, for their fall 2021 collection, created fifty of their own humanlike avatars, along with a custom video game backdrop made by Unreal Engine, to showcase the collection's neo-medieval style clothing (Samaha 2021).

Cameron-James Wilson, a professional fashion photographer who had photographed top models like Gigi Hadid, created "the world's first digital supermodel." In 2017, he quit photography, learned 3D drawing by watching YouTube videos, and created a virtual supermodel named Shudu. Within two years, she was featured in *Vogue* and *Women's Wear Daily* and amassed 240,000 Instagram followers, earning partnerships with Louis Vuitton and Balmain. Wilson has since added more virtual models and created a digital modeling agency called The Diigitals Agency (Semic 2019).

The benefits of creating or hiring virtual influencers are many. They can promote brands twenty-four seven, they don't require makeup artists, photographers, or a studio rental, and they are more flexible in where they can show up because they don't have to travel.

Virtual models won't necessarily replace real-life models, but, in fact, real-life models and celebrities are creating their own virtual avatars that are available for hire. Genies is a Los Angeles-based digital avatar start-up that has partnered with celebrities like Justin Bieber, Migo, and Cardi B, and it was already valued at $1 billion in 2022. They have expanded beyond celebrity avatars and into direct-to-consumer NFTs and digital fashion.

Genies' NFT storefront "is available to the general public, meaning users can download the Genies Studio app to create their own avatars and buy digital fashion items to dress them." The purchased digital clothing can then be customized and personalized using their app and sold as NFTs, allowing creators to monetize their creations, while Genies earns a 5 percent royalty for each sale (Matney 2022).

Akash Nigam, the CEO of Genies, also recognizes that not everyone wants to buy NFTs as investments or to gain access to special perks. Nigam, who believes his target audience wants to create great digital fashion, trade it, and collaborate with friends to create more, says, "people are just obsessed with the actual digital fashion itself and creating (their) dream closet" (Ramaswamy 2022).

The virtual realm provides many opportunities for content creators or influencers. Designers themselves can wear and promote avatar fashion, introverted individuals can transform into virtual influencers, and those with artistic talents can unleash their creativity to dream up virtual models for hire. Moreover, those who create or trade digital fashion can also build a dedicated following for their curated closet, whether or not they utilize NFTs. Once again, the potential for content creation in the virtual realm is incredibly diverse and abundant.

ARTIFICIAL INTELLIGENCE

Suppose people become obsessed with digital fashion, as Nigam suggests, and aspire to become creators. In that case, they may not necessarily need to acquire digital design skills or purchase customizable items. Thanks to the proliferation of artificial intelligence (AI), anyone with good taste and the ability to write prompts can now generate digital designs. However, this process is not as easy as it sounds.

During my initial experience with Midjourney, the AI program capable of producing stunning renderings in as little as sixty seconds, I was pleasantly surprised by the outcomes, but I was not initially blown away. I requested a romantic garden setting with a beautiful model, long wavy red hair, and a modern white gown with 3D embroidered flowers in various colors. Unfortunately, the first few attempts yielded results that were less realistic and less modern than I envisioned. It became apparent that this process required more effort than I thought.

After watching a few instructional videos on YouTube, I learned there are many specific prompts, like *photo-realistic* and *studio lighting*, that helped me get closer to what I desired. With some trial and error, the outcomes became truly incredible. As with any AI tool, the choice of prompts plays a critical role. Nevertheless, the essential point is that I didn't need traditional art supplies or the ability to develop a garment pattern to visualize my fashion ideas.

Many AI tools for creators are developing faster than we can imagine. Ivan Puzyrev, cofounder of W3rlds, a metaverse platform, demonstrated one tool for me that took a 2D flat image and, in one minute, converted it into a 3D rendering.

AI is an excellent tool for creative types to bring their ideas to life. However, it still requires a certain level of talent. It certainly allows creatives who lack drawing skills to unleash their creativity. And even for those who do have drawing skills, it allows for much more experimentation. Although the process may not be straightforward, AI serves as a powerful medium for anyone seeking creative expression to push the boundaries of their artistry.

The emerging era of the internet is giving rise to a 3D virtual world that will likely be a creator's paradise. In this new realm, we each possess our own avatars, and these avatars will wear digital fashion. Virtual worlds open up new opportunities for creators and creative individuals who acquire new skills to create and make themselves known.

Brands are already experimenting with avatars, virtual models, NFTs, and digital fashion. And this new world opens up opportunities for many more creators to become digital fashion designers, avatar designers, NFT creators, gallery or boutique owners, virtual influencers, and likely additional types of fashion creators we haven't thought of yet.

The future belongs to those who dare to embrace this transformative digital frontier and use their creativity to make their mark on a world of limitless possibilities.

PART IV

A BRAND PERSPECTIVE

CHAPTER 9

BENEFITS FOR BUSINESS

Understand what the state of the art is for your industry, for your company. Otherwise, you risk being disrupted.

—JEFF WONG, GLOBAL CHIEF INNOVATION OFFICER, EY

To fully understand the Metaverse's potential benefits to the bottom line, we must first take a look at today's pain points that many fashion brands share.

Currently, fashion brands face many common challenges that lead to underwhelming revenue and unsustainable practices. The pain points causing these challenges persist despite macroeconomic trends. For one, captivating customers' attention and building loyalty amidst all the noise out there becomes increasingly difficult. It has also become commonplace for fashion brands to witness only a fraction of their items generate the majority of demand, jeopardizing their revenue and resulting in excess inventory. The production process poses its own challenges, with high sample expenses and a lengthy fashion calendar that leads to overproduction and high levels of waste.

Much of these challenges can be attributed to the e-commerce model, which prioritizes search results over thoughtful curation. Unfortunately, this model and these brand-specific pain points also result in customer pain points—feeling overwhelmed by too many choices, frustrated with too many returns, and concerned about the environmental impact that excessive shipping causes.

The encouraging news is that a 3D internet channel, and even the preparation for one, can likely address many of these challenges and even enhance e-commerce performance. In this chapter, we'll dive into how the immersive web featuring curated assortments can effectively engage customers, foster loyalty, and potentially boost sales, reduce return rates, and improve inventory management. We will also delve into the advantages of preparing for a 3D internet by shifting the design and production process to utilizing realistic 3D assets, which can result in considerable time and cost savings throughout the fashion calendar process. The Web 3.0 era presents numerous compelling advantages for brands to seize.

CUSTOMER LOYALTY AND ENGAGEMENT
Allow me to paint a picture of a brand that captivated my attention in its immersive experience. Stepping into Hugo Boss's vast metaverse showroom, a well-lit space of neutral tones, I was drawn to an iridescent floating orb in the distance. I walked along a tranquil reflecting pool, passing other visitors, and the moment I approached the orb, it gracefully ascended into the open sky. Hovering in that spot was a white tailored suit from the runway. As I was proceeding up the grand stone staircase and admiring other runway looks in the virtual environment, I discovered more orbs that, upon final activation, rewarded me with a digital suit for my avatar. Although the space was sparse and the looks somewhat limited (these are the early days, after all), I found myself thoroughly engaged, leisurely exploring my surroundings, and seeking out the orbs within this immersive world.

According to data from metaverse builder Emperia, retailers found that users spend an average of fourteen minutes interacting with a brand's virtual experience compared to two minutes in their

2D stores (Dogadkina 2022). From my personal encounter, I can comprehend the reasons behind this. The metaverse experience considerably slowed down my pace compared to my swift reactions to social media posts or scrolling on conventional websites.

Another compelling advantage of an immersive internet will be the ability for a brand to have the presence of stylists or sales associates. Imagine that customers can try clothing on their avatar, weeding out some choices, and a stylist can make suggestions, reducing some of the returns caused by try-ons at home. We are in a very early stage; however, we can envision the immense impact human interaction will have when it eventually becomes a part of these experiences. Studies show that consumers across various industries crave more genuine human interaction than they currently get from most companies.

A report by PwC revealed that 82 percent of US consumers desire more human interaction in the future, with 59 percent of all consumers feeling that companies have lost touch with the human element of customer service. Customers are more likely to stay loyal to a brand if they have positive experiences (PwC 2023). The potential of the 3D internet to foster loyalty through engaging activities and human interaction will also likely lead to higher conversion, as it does in physical stores. And this leads us to another benefit of the immersive channel—new revenue streams.

NEW REVENUE STREAMS

There are several opportunities for new revenue streams in the immersive internet channel, including digital fashion, phygital fashion, and NFTs, as well as e-commerce and store sales generated from the virtual channel.

Digital fashion, for dressing our avatars, is a key opportunity, and it can also be tied to physical twins. Within one year of launching virtual products in their metaverse store in *Roblox*, Forever 21's virtual beanie hat, priced at seventy cents, had sold one million units and cost only $500 to produce (Business Wire 2022). It was then produced in physical form for $14.99, along with physical hoodies and tees that were added in the same aesthetic (AN Editorial Staff 2022). This example of phygital fashion—virtual items with matching physical twins—is a type of product testing that Forever 21 plans to repeat (Klasa 2023).

Metaverse fashion could generate $55 billion by 2030 (Deloitte 2022). In my conversation with Daria Shapovalova, the founder of DRESSX, the digital fashion marketplace, she shared their collaborative efforts with brands to develop versatile digital fashion pieces. Once designing an item into a digital format, they can transform it to serve a multitude of purposes across various platforms—for dressing avatars in virtual realms, for augmented reality experiences, and as collectibles, or NFTs—each leading to a potential revenue stream.

Just like in the physical world, self-expression remains a driving force in the virtual realm. In the future, we can likely expect to have to attend virtual events and dress up for them. Brands have the opportunity to pair digital fashion with physical twins, creating a potentially lucrative avenue for expanding business in other channels as well.

Nike x Gucci collaborated on a sweatshirt that had a special label with a QR code. The video ad for this caramel-colored hoody shows the male model reaching down to the banded bottom of the hoody to take a picture of the QR code. The link on his phone then leads him to a virtual "twin" of the same sweatshirt, a digital asset he has just acquired with his physical purchase. With this new virtual hoody, he gets the option to put it on his avatar, and voilà, he is his online self, ready to explore the Metaverse. This example of phygital fashion, beginning with the physical item, is yet another way to generate new demand and engage the customer in the process.

Charli Cohen, a designer who launched her "multiverse" collection, RSTLSS, has partnerships with Epic Games, *Roblox*, and Paris Hilton. She found that users want to express themselves in metaverse worlds just as they do in real life. Her collection pulls from Web3 tech to provide digital counterparts to physical fashion. Consumers can experience this in AR, VR, online games, and the Metaverse (Ginsberg 2022).

Customized avatars are another revenue opportunity for brands and retailers. Charlotte Tilbury, the beauty brand, experimented with runway-ready avatars that mirrored the makeup looks of campaign ambassadors, including Jourdan Dunn and Kate Moss (Obsess 2023). Ready Player Me, the avatar platform, offers many standard looks that a user can choose at no cost, but brands can partner with Ready Player Me to create specialized avatar attributes that some fans are willing to pay for. AI can also take customization to a new level, allowing customers to create their own look, which Ready Player Me has already introduced.

NFTs can be a lucrative source of revenue for the creator, generating income during their origin—minting—and initial sale, as well as with every future transaction in the secondary market. As discussed earlier, NFTs are digital assets stored on the blockchain that can provide compelling perks, like memberships, enabling brands to engage with customers in new ways. The utility of NFTs continues to progress. A newer type, dynamic NFT, can change even after it's purchased, giving customers surprises that continue to delight and engage them. For example, creators can program a dynamic NFT to alter its colors every month or showcase other innovative variations the creator comes up with. It is evident that these digital assets will evolve in exciting and imaginative ways and gain even more popularity.

Upselling becomes a distinct advantage of virtual shopping spaces because brand associates or AI assistants could offer styling advice and interact directly with shoppers. This is a major differentiating factor that is not readily available in 2D platforms. The social feature of a virtual store will more closely mirror a physical store, but the virtual store has the added benefit of providing experiences that are not possible in a physical space. For example, picture a customer who is shopping for a vacation in the South of France and suddenly finds themselves in a "fitting room" that transforms into a breathtaking terrace overlooking the Mediterranean Sea. Imaginative ideas abound in the 3D immersive shopping channel.

Multi-brand retailers with virtual stores provide another revenue stream for brands and for themselves. They can potentially partner with brands in exciting ways, displaying unique brand boutiques or leasing space. In common areas, these retailers can create captivating displays that combine different brands' products, giving inspiration to shoppers, much like they do in physical store setups. Leveraging AI, it even becomes possible to generate customized displays that change in real-time based on the individual shopper present. These scenarios present revenue streams for both the multi-brand retailers and the brands.

These immersive shopping experiences naturally extend to increased sales in physical stores by offering customers the option to purchase physical items. By bridging the gap between physical and virtual realms, virtual shopping spaces unlock many possibilities for both customers and brands alike.

REDUCING TIMELINE AND WASTE
Beginning with the end in mind can benefit brands in various ways. A 3D store requires 3D digital assets. A brand that undergoes a digital transformation to utilize 3D assets as part of its workflow now, will be better prepared when the time comes to launch a 3D virtual store. Three-dimensional assets provide benefits that save time and money

in all three phases of the fashion calendar—design and development, sell-in, and production.

I recall being in a sample meeting for a brand's collection. I was seated on one side of a large horseshoe as a few models waited to start the internal fashion show. Several weeks prior, the designers had presented the sketches in the same room. The sketches were based on the merchants' line plans, and the team had curated which sketches to turn into samples. The last of the samples, which took longer than usual, had arrived from China the day before.

The merchants and product developers now sat with the 14" x 17" multipage line plans, which the designers had updated with the chosen sketches. The dark-haired model floated in. She was wearing the first item on the plan, which was a cream-colored, spaghetti-strapped, fitted crepe dress that flared at the knee. The fabric draped beautifully, and it looked even better than the sketch. The next model, wearing a cotton cropped top and skirt set, was tugging at a seam and looked very uncomfortable. The items in the set looked nothing like the sketch, and the designer commented that she almost decided not to present them.

The merchants had planned the two-piece outfit as a "high-potential" look based on the trending data and beautiful sketch. Sadly, it had sampled much stiffer in real life because the fabric didn't drape the way the designer had expected it to. The room turned quiet because we knew the calendar was running very late, and we could not develop a replacement in time.

Flat sketches and even illustrations sometimes fail to accurately represent the final product. Had the team used 3D software with a fabric library to design this item, they would have identified the issue sooner. The brand would have saved time and money that could have been used for another sample. By utilizing 3D design software in the design and development phase, design teams can achieve more accurate designs and gain more opportunities for experimentation. This approach, in turn, enables more time for merchandising teams to strategically build high-performing assortments, likely benefitting the overall financial results.

In the next phase of the fashion calendar, or the sell-in phase, hyper-realistic 3D assets that replace showroom samples for buyers to edit from can also shorten the fashion calendar. During the pandemic, when travel was more difficult, and remote buying became the norm, some brands and retailers bought from 3D assets. However, now more than ever, 3D sales samples remain an option that could save time and expense, particularly for a brand's foundational or nonfashion items.

During our conversation, Christopher Screnci, a highly experienced head of product development and sourcing, offered invaluable insights. With a deep background working for notable brands such as The Gap and Levi's, he highlighted the positive impact of making the switch to 3D sales samples at one particular brand. This change resulted in substantial benefits for the company. By shifting 40 percent of the SKUs in the sales rep sample collection to 3D versions only, they reduced sample expenses by $2.5 million, lowered their product development costs by 5 percent to 15 percent, and achieved a remarkable three-to-four-month reduction in their go-to-market timeline. Such substantial time and cost savings directly contributed to the bottom line, reinforcing the positive impact of leveraging 3D technology in the industry.

For the third phase—production—manufacturers can become more efficient by adopting 3D technology for fitting garments. During my conversation with Yelena Mogelefsky, senior vice president of production at Komar, an apparel manufacturer, she shared a notable insight about the use of 3D technologies by their production teams. Specifically, 3D technologies have enabled faster and more accurate garment fits, as well as streamlined the size grading process.

By leveraging these advanced tools, they have successfully reduced production timelines by several weeks.

Anne-Christine Polet, whom I also spoke with, was SVP leading innovation for PVH, the parent company of Tommy Hilfiger and Calvin Klein. She and her team later developed Stitch, a 3D software platform that has become its own spin-off company. She believes 3D design helps brands in two ways. For brands with an innovation mindset, thinking about Web 3.0 and the Metaverse, 3D design is what Polet calls an "on-ramp" to the Metaverse. For brands that are just concerned with getting through the current season's calendar, 3D technology helps them simplify, with less manual work, and is "future-proofing" them for the long term.

Whether a company adopts 3D technology for one phase in the process or for all of it, the resulting reduction in expenses, time, and waste can be significant. However, as with any major change, there are trade-offs to consider. Brand merchants and designers used to seeing physical samples of every style may not trust 3D samples to work for their needs. Nevertheless, there are additional benefits that merchandising can derive from utilizing 3D samples. By editing the assortment earlier, merchants gain time to plan strategically, which can help the next pain point—excess inventory.

IMPROVED INVENTORY MANAGEMENT

When I delve into analyzing a fashion business for the first time, one aspect that never fails to excite me is the ranked selling report. I love knowing what products the brand is best at. Recently, while reading such a report, I experienced the usual thrill upon seeing a best-selling item that generated eight figures in revenue in just one season. However, as I scanned the full report, I noted the exceptionally "long tail" of slow sellers. These items had fallen into the trap of either "too much of a good thing" or "too much of the wrong attribute." Consequently, the brand dealt with excess inventory. The dead stock included items that had already lived through a long fashion calendar after being turned into multiple samples—for fittings, showroom sales, and photography. These underperforming products had taken up many peoples' time and incurred substantial expenses for the brand.

There's a reason why so many brands are "just concerned with getting through the season's calendar." They are often dealing with the many challenges of running an apparel business today, especially one that is heavily dependent on the e-commerce model and its inventory requirements. A start-up founder of a high-growth, digitally native brand admitted they generate 90 percent of their sales on less than 10 percent of their items.

I spoke to one COO of a notable fashion e-commerce retailer, who was a former executive at a major department store, and he reflected, "the number one challenge in the industry is inventory"—and the e-commerce model has made inventory a bigger challenge than ever before. The COO explained that having a greater variety of items increases a brand's online presence, but none of the items are differentiated on the page. For this reason, and due to minimums, many of the items are bought in equal amounts, regardless of their projected sales. This scenario leads to too many "overbought" items and a glut of inventory, which is unsustainable.

Another challenge for brands is that multi-brand retailers have now adopted a marketplace model, similar to Amazon, where third-party vendors can "sell" on the retailer's website and pay a royalty for that privilege. This creates more competition for the brands and more work for the consumer. The customer has many more choices, which makes it harder to find the right item and more likely for them to abandon the search. This adds to the inventory problem.

There is hope for dramatically improved inventory management in the new immersive channel of the Metaverse. A virtual store mirrors a physical store more closely than it does an online store. Because of the virtual realm's shopping format, merchandising becomes more strategic and curated, compared to todays' online stores, where they treat items as equals.

So, how does this help the inventory problem? By 2030, McKinsey estimates that "more than 80 percent of commerce could be impacted by something consumers do (in the Metaverse), from discovering brands to visiting a virtual store" (McKinsey & Company 2022). Merchandising that is strategic and curated results in fewer items and inventory can be bought with more conviction versus the online model. The shift to a 3D internet will likely lead to better curation for all channels, more strategic buying, and an improvement in inventory performance—one of the biggest challenges in fashion commerce today.

The Metaverse commerce model has the potential to provide multiple benefits to the bottom line. More interactive customer engagement can increase conversion and lower return rates. Three-dimensional digital assets can save time and cut costs on the fashion calendar, from the design phase to the selling phase and even e-commerce. New revenue streams emerge, such as 3D digital fashion for avatars, NFTs, and upselling in a new channel. A curated assortment can potentially drive more revenue on fewer styles, improving inventory challenges and mitigating sustainability issues. The promise of the Metaverse gives us much to look forward to in potential process improvement, increased revenue, and profitability.

CHAPTER 10

RISKS AND THE COST OF INACTION

By 2005 or so, it will become clear that the Internet's impact on the economy has been no greater than the fax machine's.
—PAUL KRUGMAN, NOBEL PRIZE ECONOMIST, SAID BACK IN 1998

During the exciting yet uncertain times of the early tech boom in 1999, I found myself working at a dot com start-up. I was at Saks Fifth Avenue when the parent company formed a separate, new start-up division to build and launch the retailer's dot com. The three founding members of the team, former executives from consulting and operations, were instructed not to "poach" anyone from the internal talent pool. But I made my case to join them.

Back then, it was not a popular career choice in our industry. I vividly remember a respected senior executive, who was thirty years my senior, confidentially telling me, "Between you and me, this project is going to fail. No one will buy luxury online."

I made up my mind and felt relieved when I got the job to lead merchandising for the start-up. We started from scratch with no playbook, but we had a dedicated floor, a blank whiteboard with erasable markers, and our passionate energy. Together, we brainstormed, defined our strategic vision, and built the structure of our teams. We collaborated with an external agency to build our website, learning new things every day and interviewing potential team members regularly. Within a year, we formed an internal team of 110, and the intense journey continued.

The morning after the website launch day, we couldn't get to the reports fast enough to see which products had sold. We were intrigued that shoes were the star category of day one. However, in that same year, a devastating economic event sent shockwaves across the country. The dot-com bubble burst. The atmosphere changed around us, and we had to swiftly adapt when the agency we had been working with folded.

During the development phase, I often wondered how customers would find items buried on page 10 of our listings. I sensed that marketing efforts would need to focus on an item level. In year one, we tested a lot and learned a lot, as the orders came in slower than our predictions with no historical context. It took time for this new channel to find its rhythm, and the role that digital marketing would play was yet to be determined.

On February 14, 2001, I faced one of the toughest challenges of my career. Presented with a lengthy list of names, I had the task of laying off members of our talented team. Was the leader who said no one would buy luxury online correct? No, time would prove he was mistaken. As with any digital disruption, results don't happen overnight. Customers gradually got comfortable buying clothes in this new way. Within about two years, they called back and rehired many of those laid off.

Embarking on a new start-up venture is like riding a roller coaster, even for a legacy institution. However, in my professional opinion, the CEO of the parent company, R. Brad Martin, made a brilliant move by prioritizing e-commerce and assembling a dedicated team free from the constraints of existing operations. He understood the importance of building a best-in-class dot-com presence from the outset, with the ability to iterate and adapt rather than piecemeal efforts pulled in different directions. Our digital transformation involved taking risks and learning from our mistakes, but ultimately, it proved to be very successful.

It's crucial to acknowledge that technological advancements, including Web 3.0 and the Metaverse, bring inherent risks, particularly considering the added social component that distinguishes this channel from traditional online stores. Although many of the risks mirror the first internet era, there are also new sustainability issues, heightened cybersecurity risks, and people with bad intentions. Fashion brands should not overlook these risks, and we will go through them in this chapter. However, it's equally important to recognize the costs of inaction. Not every path is right for everyone, so carefully weighing the risks against the consequences of inaction is essential before deciding where to start.

RISK: INVESTING EARLY CAN BE MORE COSTLY. OR NOT.
Technology advancements take time. But when they hit the inflection point, mass adoption kicks in. Take generative artificial intelligence, for example. In many ways, generative AI has been in development for over a decade. But it was only in November 2022, when ChatGPT launched, that millions of people started using it for all sorts of functions, from writing marketing emails to generating computer code.

Likewise, video games became a great testing ground for virtual worlds when 3D internet browsing was getting started in 2010 (Zdrzałek, Michalak 2021). But no one can predict exactly when the Metaverse, or a fully immersive internet, will become part of our daily lives.

Some major components need to fall into place before the Metaverse is fully developed and operable, which might happen in this decade, but it might take longer. So it may be a risk, in terms of return on investment, to invest too early. On the other hand, investing early and learning the process sooner may save money in the long run. Either way, it is advantageous to stay informed about what the latest developments are so that when they advance, the timing becomes more realistic.

Understanding what exactly these developments are about mitigates some of the uncertainty. Experts have no doubt that a 3D internet is not only possible, but it is inevitable. The timing is related to concrete factors—networks, hardware, and computing power—which will allow for the rendering and experience that will bring about mass adoption.

Let's start with networks. Today, we are in the fifth generation of wireless cellular technology, or 5G. Every ten years, our data transmission speeds have increased by twenty to fifty times. In the past decade or so, our devices have gone from having 3G, with advanced speeds for web browsing, video streaming, video calls, music streaming, and GPS, to 4G, which gave us HD video streaming, wearable devices, and high-speed apps. In 2019, 5G gave us more possibilities for cloud storage and edge computing, which is revolutionary (Drawing Capital 2020).

The Metaverse also needs to be interoperable so a user can easily go from one place to another with the same wallet, avatar, and clothing. Otherwise, it won't feel like a connected internet and will cause more frustration than pleasure. The cloud enables the large amounts of data required for our unique avatars, movements, and transactions, but there is another necessary element that a more powerful network affects—latency.

Low latency means fast reaction time. For example, if you're driving a virtual car and hit the brakes at a red light, you expect the car to stop in that millisecond. For latency to match our expectation of real-world reaction times in the Metaverse, many experts believe the network speed will require 6G. Other experts believe 5G networks combined with edge computing, which puts the cell service locally closer to the user, is enough for the Metaverse ecosystem (David 2023).

Once we do have more advanced networks, we will need upgraded devices. These may be computers, or they may be glasses or other devices we have never seen before. But, most experts believe we will move away from being dependent on our smartphones.

Most of us can recall when Google launched their glasses, and they never really took off. This was a case of hardware that came about before the networks made it worthwhile. One can say the same about the *Oculus* and *Horizon Worlds*. The advanced device has a lot of potential, but the network capabilities have not caught up to what it can do. The glitches, speed delays, and low-quality rendering of avatars make it more frustrating than enjoyable, and the repeat rate is very low.

The new Apple Vision Pro, available in 2024, is the most advanced device yet. It's a headset with 3D and full Apple computer capabilities. But, it remains to be seen how it handles the network and the 3D apps that developers will create for it. In any case, as the networks advance, those same devices will likely continue to perform better and become smaller versions, which will provide a better user experience. After all, the iPod Nano versus the iPod Classic was 76 percent smaller in volume with 35 percent higher resolution (VERSUS n.d.).

Networks and devices are critical, but computing power is probably the biggest challenge. Intel is one of the largest makers of processors that power our computers. "According to Raja Koduri, VP of Intel's accelerated computing systems and graphics group, 'powering the Metaverse will require a 1,000-fold improvement on the computational infrastructure we have today'" (Ramirez 2021). The reason for such a high requirement is the data needed for the Metaverse to run. And processing that much data brings about another issue—sustainability.

RISK: A DIFFERENT KIND OF SUSTAINABILITY ISSUE

Massive amounts of data consume enormous amounts of energy. So why is so much data required? Realistic avatars will need to have unique hair, skin, and clothing and read data from users wearing audio and motion sensors that show natural movements. Many people interacting in the same virtual world with all these unique and realistic details require enormous amounts of data in real time. Some start-ups create hyperrealistic avatars, but those avatars are not in virtual worlds in real time with many others like them. Avatars in today's virtual worlds still look "cartoony" and have limited attribute choices or stiff movements.

On the other hand, the data-heavy 3D design that more sophisticated avatars and fashion will require in virtual worlds may be offset by other sustainability benefits. Virtual fashion may lead to more on-demand production, reducing the excess merchandise that goes to the landfill. Virtual events may also shift purchases from physical to digital fashion, reducing overconsumption and resulting in a net positive effect for the planet.

Commerce in virtual worlds requires payments. The Metaverse may possibly operate in the blockchain, and on-chain transactions consume more energy than regular payments. "A single credit card transaction in real life only consumes about 149-kilowatt hours (kWh) of energy, but a transaction in the Metaverse using digital currency will consume 14 times that amount at around 2,189 kWh" (Dublin Tech Blog 2023). The good news is energy initiatives are in the process of improving the environmental impact of the blockchain (World Economic Forum 2023).

The Metaverse presents sustainability concerns. However, it is very encouraging that global organizations are actively working toward enhancing the sustainability of blockchain technology. The fashion industry stands to gain from virtual worlds because it holds the potential for on-demand production, mitigating the issue of excess production and reducing wasteful practices.

RISK: PEOPLE ONLINE WITH BAD INTENTIONS
Just as there are people with ill intentions on the internet, there will be those in the Metaverse as well, and it may be even easier for them to exploit others. Avatars who appear innocent might be the complete opposite. Terrorist groups can convene and use virtual worlds to get better at attacking or actually attack a valuable virtual world. Hackers will undoubtedly continue to attack the accounts of people who are not careful.

One advantage of decentralization lies in the ability of decentralized autonomous organizations (DAOs) to effectively monitor, police, and impose penalties on unethical entities. Additionally, government agencies are taking initiatives to regulate this space and address this very pressing need. The cybersecurity industry will become even more critical and assume more importance than it does today (Linganna 2023).

RISK: MASS ADOPTION MAY BE SLOWER THAN ANTICIPATED
Some surveys have shown that people don't want to be a part of the Metaverse. A study by Morning Consult, which surveyed 4,420 US adults about the Metaverse, found that more than half feel a major concern about the misuse of their personal data. Other major concerns include cyberbullying from 44 percent of the group and mental health impacts from 27 percent of the group (Teale 2022).

With personal data management being the top concern, it is important to note this is top of mind in the blockchain community and is part of the regulatory initiatives in work. As Hazel Evans, a leader in this space, explained, "This includes advanced protocols to keep data secure and only pass limited data to the distributed network, thus retaining a level of confidentiality."

Individuals have real and valid concerns, and we can expect that mass adoption will be bumpy and slow-moving, just as it was in the early days of the internet. But one thing we know for sure is that Gen Z embraces digital worlds, and the youngest will become adults by 2030 when the Metaverse is predicted to be up and running. This generation and Gen Alpha, the one after it, will most likely lead the way as others come on board.

RISK: LACK OF ADOPTION BY TEAMS
How a company treats a Metaverse initiative will directly affect its success with it. If it is treated like an add-on project or work for teams to take on that are already overloaded, they may get burned out and not move the progress forward. For fashion companies, there may be resistance from design teams unskilled in 3D design. Without focus, a "learn as you go" process may slow things down. What could take months might take years if it doesn't receive the right attention. The successful Saks case study of entering the World Wide Web early, swiftly, and with a focused team is worth noting.

COST OF INACTION
TIME LOST LEADS TO SCRAMBLING LATER
Putting the burden of something as big as Web 3.0 on an existing team can backfire if they get burned out or if it detracts them from their core role. A new evolution takes time, and having to start over means time is lost. On the other hand, doing nothing is also time lost and could be costly in the long run. Test and learn is the model for new technology. Not having time to test and learn means scrambling to catch up later. Building things in a rush can lead to costly mistakes or, even worse, a complete redesign in the future. Many

fashion brands made the mistake of delaying the development of their websites, and as a result, they faced costly redesigns after witnessing their e-commerce sites underperforming and failing to meet user experience expectations.

LACK OF SKILLED TALENT

With new technology requiring complex skills in 3D design, game engines, and blockchain technology, there is already a limited pool of experienced talent. We can imagine that there is plenty of demand for their work. But it pays to consider the fact that, just like every company needed to build a website, every company will need to build a virtual space. The individuals with the skills for it may be hard to come by in a few years, and the best of them will be in demand. Even if outsourcing much of the work, it is advantageous for leaders to learn the language to be able to articulate their needs.

THE COMPETITION

Brands that don't innovate die, as there will always be competitors who embrace innovation and capture market share from those who don't. It may take a decade for that to happen, but no one likes to watch a slow death. We saw it happen with countless brands that didn't embrace the new models of doing business in a digital world. Brands that did not embrace e-commerce or social media lost market share to digitally native brands. There will likely be virtual-native brands that claim market share from brands that are slow to adopt in Web 3.0.

CONCLUSION

Entering the Metaverse carries inherent risks for businesses. The timeline is uncertain, and taking the plunge creates an added expense without a clear idea of when the returns will start to come in. In my conversation with Evans, she added, "No one's talking about the profitability because it doesn't really exist yet. It will come, just as it did for e-commerce, and it will come in droves." Evans firmly believes companies will be more inclined to invest when there is more regulation, which is indeed a logical notion.

The Metaverse brings about legitimate concerns for cybersecurity, sustainability, and unresolved issues related to legal frameworks and taxation. However, proactive initiatives are already underway to address these concerns. Even when the Metaverse officially launches, we can expect mass adoption to be gradual—as it was for e-commerce. Nonetheless, we can acknowledge that progress has started, and it is growing rapidly and evolving with each passing day.

There are costs to inaction. Treating it like an add-on can impact existing teams, but doing nothing can lead to playing catch-up later. It can be extremely costly to scramble late in the game to build something that experts say will be as big as the launch of the internet and mobile smartphones. The competition may have a jump start on hiring the skilled talent, and claim market share in the new channel. Moreover, a brand that does not take action will appear to be lacking in innovation.

The bottom line is that Web 3.0 is the next era of the internet, and the components are already here. A brand can take steps to prepare. When in doubt, take it from McKinsey & Co., "The opportunity is enormous, and the risk is not what you think it is… The biggest risk is missing the wave of change that breakthrough technologies like the original internet, AI, and the Metaverse can unleash" (Hatami 2023).

CHAPTER 11

WHERE TO START

Far from disproving it, uncertainty and confusion are features of disruption.

—MATTHEW BALL, CEO, EPYLLION; AUTHOR, *THE METAVERSE*

It's hard to grasp something that does not yet exist. Today, can a nongamer imagine creating an avatar and entering a virtual world if they've never done it before? I couldn't until I actually tried it. It makes sense that businesses may find it just as hard to imagine commerce in a virtual world. But if there is one industry that this innovation will likely change, it is the fashion industry.

In this chapter, we will dive into the practical aspects of getting started. Just like a successful fashion business, building a Web 3.0 entity requires big ideas, a well-defined strategy, and compelling products. Throughout my interviews with experts for this book, a consistent message emerged: Brands should not hastily enter the Metaverse solely due to fear of missing out (FOMO). As with any disruptive change, it is crucial for organizations to prioritize education and adopt a strategic approach.

Harvard Business Review published a simple guide for embarking on this new venture, summarized in these five key points:
1. Pick your targets. If your consumer is younger, then there is less time to wait.
2. Monitor the competition.
3. Look for applications like sustainability.
4. Plan your entrance.
5. Keep your balance. Be agile and expect some failures (Balis 2022).

These valid points are generally applicable to various industries; however, my focus will be more specific to fashion and retail. The fashion industry can also benefit from a critical component not on their list—personal exploration. After all, thinking like a customer wins every time.

MINDSET

A great place to start is with a mindset shift. This includes a mindset of curiosity and understanding the *why*. Why will consumers be drawn to the Metaverse? What factors will keep them there? What innovations are already happening that solidify the Metaverse is inevitable? The encouraging news is that anyone reading this book is already in the curiosity mindset, and it is my hope that they gain a clear understanding of the answers to these fundamental questions.

A company will have many skeptics, especially if their customer is not on the younger side. And most people don't like change. Having some team members who are skeptical about the Metaverse *and* averse to change and others who are not may create more tension and confusion for the company as a whole. According to the *Harvard Business Review* guide, the most important person to set the tone is the CEO. From there, you can educate the talent and align them to be on the same page. This mirrors my experience with the advent of the original Web: the parent company CEO set the tone, and the rest of the organization followed suit at varying speeds.

JUMP IN PERSONALLY

One thing is certain. Developing a Web 3.0/Metaverse strategy will be challenging without first taking the plunge personally. Going in with the perspective of the customer is always a wise approach. To begin with, augmented reality (AR) is a relatively straightforward starting point. With just a smartphone and a mirror, one can engage in some fun experimentation with AR dressing, and if no mirror is available, a full-body selfie will suffice. Some apps and sites in which to try AR are Zero10, Snapchat's Dress Up feature, DRESSX.com, TheFabricant.com, and TheDematerialised.com.

Next, teams can create their own avatars and explore some virtual worlds, especially in the virtual platforms embraced by early adopter fashion brands. Ready Player Me—readyplayer.me—is a great avatar platform to start with because the avatars are compatible with many other platforms. It's also possible to skip that step and go directly to a platform like Spatial.io or download the *Decentraland* app to create an avatar and explore. Note that *Decentraland* operates on the blockchain and requires additional steps. This type of exploration provides a good idea of what dressing an avatar feels like and what an immersive journey will be like for a customer in the Metaverse.

PRODUCT FIRST: THINK IN 3D

Fashion brands and retailers can take steps toward embracing a Web 3.0 future even before a vision for the Metaverse has been set because we know we are moving toward a 3D internet. There are different approaches to bringing 3D design into the equation. One is investing in 3D software, such as Clo or Browzwear, and upskilling the design team by training some individuals in 3D design, or bringing on board a 3D digital designer to convert 2D designs into 3D versions. Another option is outsourcing this work to a third party specializing in digital asset preparation.

For upskilling the team, a member of The Fabricant team explains that digital fashion has a short learning curve and doesn't require being good at drawing, and "You can learn in three months without being a tailor" (Hecker 2022). I asked several sources about outsourcing digital assets. Depending on the complexity, it can cost between $500 to a few thousand for each, so it can be very valuable to upskill the team.

As Adriana Hoppenbrouwer-Pereira, cofounder of The Fabricant, explained so directly, "3D digital design is a no-brainer from the simple reduction point of view—supply chain improvements, time to market, it checks so many boxes… and then you open up the world of possibilities for Web 3.0."

Once a brand has created a catalog of its 3D digital assets, the hard part is done. But there is another step to get the files ready for the Metaverse. This next step is converting the files to make them avatar ready or to enable them for the blockchain. For this, there are software subscription services, and start-ups like Stitch, The Fabricant, or DRESSX are ready to help. As Shapovalova explained, it's important to note that, currently, different virtual world platforms require different file types, with the exception of those that can utilize Ready Player Me files. Though, in a future state, the hope is that one file standard will be adopted for the entire interoperable Metaverse.

Brands that have yet to explore artificial intelligence (AI) may benefit from trying out AI bots like Midjourney, which can enhance creativity and accelerate speed to market. Some designers may have concerns about AI replacing humans who work in design, but as Rupert Breheny, Google technical specialist in AI-augmented creativity, recently told *Vogue Business*, AI is not for an unskilled person. "That person has to know the industry inside out and know how to express ideas in a way that is meaningful for the art" (McDowell 2023).

AI is a massive time-saver and enables the creation of imagery and fashion that isn't possible in the physical world (Schulz 2023). As the demand for 3D assets grows over time, it may become challenging to keep up without AI assistance, although this remains to be seen. In terms of getting started with 3D digital assets, regardless of a company's chosen path, and with or without the help of AI, incorporating these 3D assets into the process will be a significant step toward understanding the future requirements of the 3D internet channel.

Lastly, let's touch on the topic of NFTs. As discussed earlier, NFTs rely on blockchain technology, which has a learning curve. While they are a compelling option for certain brands, it's worth considering alternative starting points for exploring metaverse experiences that are less complex for the consumer, which we will delve into below.

PLAN THE ENTRANCE

Once the CEO is fully committed and ready, the crucial first step is to build a concrete metaverse strategy and craft the entry. Setting realistic expectations about the return on investment is important because the initial benefits may be more about enhancing customer engagement.

As highlighted earlier, some brands' initial entries revolved around educating consumers, such as sharing the company's history and founder story or highlighting sustainability efforts. For others, the focus was on gamification or showcasing products through a campaign or fashion show.

The approach can range from something as small as testing avatar fashion to something as substantial as creating an immersive world with phygital products, with a goal of generating revenue from both digital and physical twin fashion. In my conversations with Olivier Moingeon and Sara Texeira, executives from Metaverse agency

Exclusible, they described various brand projects they have undertaken. This included the Hugo Boss experience I explored, which Moingeon said took them forty-five days to complete. They've produced immersive experiences for shopping, customer engagement like quests, treasure hunts, or mini-games, and even work campuses for employees. The Metaverse provides many options to get started.

Even before formulating a comprehensive strategy, it is valuable to initiate regularly scheduled discussions about the actions other brands are taking, challenges that arise, and examples resonating with customers.

Monitoring the ongoing collaborations between brands and Metaverse builders can provide valuable insights. Acknowledging that there may be some setbacks when venturing into uncharted territory is important. By beginning with a customer engagement strategy, a brand can foster growth among existing customers, reignite lapsed customers, and even attract new ones. If ROI is absolutely imperative, it may be best to focus on building digital assets and decide on the right time to enter.

EXECUTING THE METAVERSE EXPERIENCE
Once a brand or retailer has decided to embark on a metaverse journey and formed a vision and high-level strategy, the next step is to decide how. The path forward is full of choices and complexities, and a consultant can be a guide, even before setting the strategy, to steer them through the many options.

One crucial factor to consider is whether to utilize a decentralized platform or not. Decentralized platforms like *Decentraland* or *The Sandbox* leverage the power of blockchain technology. As the future interoperable Metaverse may be built on the blockchain, experimenting with decentralized platforms at this stage provides brands with a valuable head start, potentially saving the time required to transition later. However, it's important to note that the user base currently on blockchain-based platforms is relatively smaller compared to the larger user populations found in certain centralized off-chain platforms.

Platforms such as Spatial and W3rlds are not blockchain-based, and they provide an alternative solution for experimenting with immersive experiences without requiring customers to own a crypto wallet. The same applies to gaming platforms like *Roblox, Fortnite,* and *Minecraft.* Although gaming platforms have a much larger user base, they currently come with certain limitations, such as the inability to integrate external avatars like those from Ready Player Me; however, this may change.

A higher-budget option is to build a white-glove streaming experience that directly links from the brand's website. Numerous agencies specialize in this area, and they continuously expand their services. For example, Journee has built and hosted high-quality experiences for brands like Clinique and H&M, while Emperia has done the same for brands like Burberry and Bloomingdale's. Agencies that build experiences hosted on multiple platforms can also partner with platforms like Journee or Emperia to host a custom white-glove experience of the highest quality.

In conversations with leaders from various platforms and agencies, I've discovered many are adopting a Web 2.5 strategy. They recognize that blockchain technology still represents challenges for the majority of consumers. Therefore, they are creating scenarios that are more centralized but can offer options, like NFTs linked to the blockchain. I spoke with Joaquin Tusquets, who advises such a platform, Algoritcom. Their plan is to onboard brands with hyperrealistic virtual worlds on a centralized platform and gradually guide them through the evolution of the technology, potentially transitioning into decentralization as the technology progresses. As per Hoppenbrouwer-Pereira, The Fabricant has also expanded its offering to include chain-agnostic options for brands that aim to progress in phases, in line with customer adoption.

For brands that have formulated a vision and are looking to enter immersive worlds, there are various entry points to consider that can be on-chain or off-chain. Whether they choose a gaming platform with a substantial audience, an immersive world platform with extensive customization, or a top-tier stand-alone streaming experience, all these options are excellent ways to prepare for the inevitable digital disruption that lies ahead. Enlisting the services of an agency to refine the strategy and craft the metaverse experience is an ideal way to make the leap. Engaging a consultant who can understand the brand's vision and objectives will be instrumental in selecting the right agency to bring that vision to life.

COMMERCE MINDSET
Customer engagement serves as a promising entry point for brands venturing into the Metaverse, but ultimately, the Metaverse represents an extraordinary opportunity as a groundbreaking new channel for shopping in this imminent era of commerce. According to McKinsey, the market impact of the Metaverse is expected to reach a staggering $4 trillion to $5 trillion by 2030, with Goldman Sachs estimating an even higher figure of $8 trillion. Of these numbers, the commerce aspect is anticipated to account for about half (McKinsey & Company 2022, Glover 2022). For the fashion industry alone, estimates amount to $55 billion by 2030 (Deloitte 2022).

Keeping this in mind, we can start to imagine the potential that the Metaverse possesses to transform intimate customer experiences into tangible revenue streams. Currently, we can identify opportunities for digital and phygital fashion, avatars, NFTs, and crossover to other channels from inspiration in the virtual space. And, of course, there are going to be other opportunities that we cannot yet imagine.

Embracing a product-centric approach and embarking on a digital transformation to 3D design gives brands a competitive advantage. This strategic shift becomes the key to best position brands to unlock their full potential in the future era of commerce, where the Metaverse captivates consumers' attention and engagement.

BE AGILE

Throughout the journey, starting from personal exploration to formulating the strategy for customer engagement or commerce and ultimately launching a metaverse experience, one thing remains undeniable: Agility is of paramount importance. Over the past two decades of digital disruption, most brands have learned the vital lesson of being agile and iterative.

There will be mistakes and even some failures, but all are necessary stepping stones for evolution. The key ingredient for embracing agility is attitude. We must wholeheartedly believe that Web 3.0 represents a superior internet and what was always meant to be for the fashion industry. It will require constant testing, learning, refining, and adapting, which is a continuous iterative process that leads us to a more immersive way of shopping and customer-brand engagement.

Through agility, we progress in an uncertain world toward an uncertain outcome. However, the best starting point is a firm belief in the awe-inspiring nature of new technologies and their ability to enhance our lives. This unwavering belief and our ability to remain agile fuels our journey in our pursuit of transformation.

CHAPTER 12

CONCLUSION

It's okay to be skeptical… but don't turn your eye on the future.
—LAURIE SEGALL, FORMER TECH CORRESPONDENT, CNN;
FOUNDER, MOSTLY HUMAN MEDIA

When the Web first launched, it changed the world forever. It gave us the conveniences of shopping, searching, learning, and connecting, among many other life-changing benefits that are too many to mention. For the fashion industry, it was also a spectacular and robust way to provide assortment breadth for the shopper.

The shopping convenience and the fashion choices we have today are unprecedented. But today's e-commerce model lacks inspiration, outfit styling, a human connection, and a social factor. The limitless amount of space, or pages, on a website, has led to too many choices, as well as other challenges for both the consumer and the brand or retailer. It has become tedious to scroll through endless pages of boxes and squares. The item-driven model creates even more work for the shopper if they want to put outfits together. For the brand or retailer, this business model makes all items appear equal, which leads to an inventory challenge because only a small percentage of the items perform exceptionally well.

Web 2.0 brought about social media, which helped generate demand for select, featured products that may have been lost in online pages. Social media has shown us that people crave inspiration, outfits, and community, and they are happy to get all that, even without seeing the outfits on supermodels. They crave ideas for how items work together to create "fits," as evidenced by the hundreds of millions of views for hashtags like #OOTD and #GRWM.

Social media has continued to evolve, and the shopping experience has evolved along with it, with platforms like TikTok becoming successful commerce platforms. Though people prefer shopping in physical stores, which provide inspiration, assistance, and the ability to shop with friends, it's not always practical. It doesn't provide the conveniences of shopping online, and our time has shifted to digital spaces. The time each new generation spends in digital spaces has increased over time, and it's not just for shopping and social media.

The newer generations are virtual world natives. As the gaming world has advanced, and with the added boost of pandemic quarantines, a vast proportion of young people have spent time in these 3D parts of the internet or virtual worlds. They've become very comfortable in their digital identities as avatars—playing, socializing, and shopping in virtual spaces.

Self-expression is just as important to users in virtual worlds as it is in the real world. Hair, makeup, jewelry, and tattoos are all ways to achieve self-expression, but none are as versatile as clothing. Clothing allows people to express their individuality. The apparel market in the US is forecast at 1.7 trillion dollars for 2023 (Gaubys 2023). And in gaming, skins already make up a $50 billion industry (Naysmith 2022). From *Roblox* to *Fortnite* and *Minecraft,* users have been spending on their digital identities even before any established fashion brands stepped in.

People want to show up in a certain way, whether it is in real life or a virtual world. As long as there are community gatherings and social events, people will attend and dress up for them. A compelling aspect of virtual worlds is that consumers can be more experimental with their digital identities without worrying about fit and modesty. A 3D immersive internet is the natural evolution of the internet. Web 3.0 and the Metaverse will once again improve our lives, as Web 1.0 and Web 2.0 did.

Some fashion leaders are still skeptical of the Metaverse. After noting disappointing results from Meta's *Horizon Worlds,* they may question its market potential, but it's crucial to consider the context. Meta's virtual world encountered setbacks, including bugs and glitches, and it currently requires the purchase of an expensive VR headset (Bastian 2022).

If we look at the success of the gaming industry and seek to understand why its appeal extends far beyond playing games, the validation of the Metaverse potential becomes quite apparent.

For many, gaming is their social platform. Many of us didn't have virtual games when we were growing up, but *Roblox* has been building communities for over a decade and has over sixty million daily active users. They are connecting, socializing, creating, and expressing themselves through digital fashion, which they are spending money on.

Some people may believe these shoppers are spending money on items that don't exist, but we are learning that a virtual existence is still an existence. In fact, *Roblox* has stated that the most popular experiences are those "that simulate real-life activities such as school and family" (Roblox 2022).

A virtual world is called a world because it allows us to move through it as we do in the real world, except it's virtual. And it does not require a headset. By creating an avatar, we can immerse ourselves and move through spaces online, feeling like we are really there. This is closer to reality, and it's more natural in how we behave than scrolling through pages on a website.

Gaming is only one example of virtual reality. In fact, virtual reality is all around us, and when done right, people can feel real emotions in those experiences, as we encountered in the ABBA Voyage show. We also reviewed earlier how virtual reality is used in areas like real estate, aviation, and as digital twins for airports and workplaces.

We encountered virtual reality for branding experiences, such as in the beautiful example from Dior Beauty. All these various use cases help us understand the vast potential for VR retail experiences in the Metaverse, as virtual reality is likely to replace some of the time we spend "surfing the web" or scrolling on social media.

Web 3.0 includes various technologies that will converge in the Metaverse. These include virtual reality and other extended realities, AI, as well as blockchain technology and NFTs. These technologies, which play a role in digital fashion and commerce, are advancing with each passing day.

Some fashion brands have proven that users are not only buying virtual goods but are also buying physical versions of them as well. We've seen phygital examples from Forever 21, Lacoste, and RTFKT x Nike. Augmented reality is already present on social media platforms and in digital fashion marketplaces like DRESSX and Zero10. Fashion NFTs provide revenue streams that keep on providing to their creators. They have been developed by countless brands as well as digitally native designer marketplaces like The Fabricant.

The Metaverse's market impact on e-commerce is expected to be over $2 trillion by 2030. What will drive mass adoption of the Metaverse? If we compare online shopping to what today's virtual worlds provide, we can begin to understand just how compelling the Metaverse can be.

People want community and connectivity, and they can get some of that through social media. But when it comes to fashion, they also want to be inspired, try on themselves, and shop with or get opinions from friends. Fashion is the ultimate form of self-expression, and we know from gaming that we can achieve this virtually. As a matter of fact, fashion inspiration, trying on "looks," and shopping with another person can all be achieved in a virtual world.

If all these benefits will exist in the Metaverse, it makes an excellent case for why the fashion consumer will be there. After all, people still prefer to shop in person, but they don't always have the time or means to get there.

Digital fashion will be one of the dominant revenue streams for fashion brands in a virtual world. This opens up a new product category with fewer barriers to entry than physical fashion. And this means endless opportunities for creators.

Fashion has always been about moving forward and innovating, and it is an art. Some fashion designers and leaders are protective of the craftsmanship and materials of physical fashion and do not embrace technology. But the world is moving in this direction, and those who embrace the technology will have a competitive advantage. Technology also provides another benefit for fashion brands—a faster speed-to-market. This holds true for both physical and digital fashion. Another technology, artificial intelligence, helps turn creative ideas into visuals in seconds. Creators with talent and taste can build digital portfolios with those visuals and some 3D software without any drawing skills. And digital styles can be converted to physical garments faster than today's processes of flat sketching.

The future demand for digital fashion in the Metaverse makes it a creator's paradise, and there are many benefits for both consumers and brands. Consumers will benefit from the entertainment, community, and convenience of all that Web 3.0 provides, including the ownership factor that blockchain technology will bring.

Brands stand to benefit from increased customer engagement and loyalty and various new revenue streams, including digital fashion, avatars, NFTs, physical fashion, and others we haven't thought of yet. Brands will also gain the added benefits that 3D assets provide in reducing timelines, expenses, and excess waste, which benefit the bottom line.

Merchandising will become a bigger focus because a virtual boutique is much more like a physical store, and brands can tell stories and showcase curated assortments. Curated assortments require more strategic buying versus today's e-commerce buying model. Shifting inventory investment to accommodate a curated assortment can reduce the number of items needed overall, improving inventory performance and profitability. Brands can stand for something and place buys in a smarter way, which can also benefit the bottom line.

The Metaverse promises to provide many benefits to the top and bottom lines. But, as with any technology, there are risks. A digital transformation and jumping into a new channel also causes disruption in the workplace. Some people will be more adaptable than others. Budgets will have to be addressed and possibly shifted, and early investments require a trial-and-error period. Risks associated with sustainability and payments—relating to blockchain—are being addressed in the cryptocurrency space. As with any new technology, there are always cybersecurity risks and people with bad intentions.

But the biggest risk comes from inaction. Slow adoption means not having the right people in place when the time comes, and it can lead to scrambling to produce a rushed metaverse experience that will have to be redone later. It could also mean losing market share to competitors who innovate sooner. In the worst case, fashion brands that wait too long may not recover, as happened with the first and second internet revolutions.

So, where should a fashion brand start? It starts with a mindset of growth and innovation and understanding the *whys*. Once a fashion brand CEO is on board with moving forward, the next step is assessing the target audience. If it makes sense to appeal to Gen Z, then a gaming platform might be the answer. If the goal is to dip a toe into digital fashion before creating a full experience, perhaps trying avatar fashion or augmented reality is a good start.

For a fashion brand ready to create a metaverse experience, perhaps it can be something temporary that takes the place of an in-person event. This type of brand experience can be a way to educate a brand's top customers, for whom it may be their first entry into the Metaverse.

Regardless of the choice, in the beginning, it will require working with a third party. And it's important to note that digital fashion assets are an added layer to the budget. A brand that already creates its own digital assets can focus more of the budget on the virtual brand experience itself.

The good news is that there are many start-ups in the space, and they each have their strengths. One way to compare them is to compile a table of early adopter fashion brands, list who they worked with, and how those experiences align with the brand's vision.

Web 3.0 is what's next for the internet, what's next for our identities, and what's next for fashion. For a fashion brand, a fashion creator, and a fashion consumer, it is not a question of whether to pursue an entry into this new channel; it is a question of when. And for something this inevitable, with many levels to choose from, there is no time like the present to take that first step.

ACKNOWLEDGMENTS

When I first discovered NFTs and the Metaverse, it felt like someone handed me a precious and unexpected gift. I never imagined the possibility of witnessing, within my lifetime, another groundbreaking transformation as profound as the original World Wide Web—a transformation that enables a whole new form of artistic expression and design.

I've always loved researching innovation, but I never fathomed that this pursuit could turn into a book, or that writing a book would be one of the most gratifying experiences in my life. I have Eric Koester and Manuscripts Modern Author Accelerator to thank for that, along with the expertise of Shanna Heath, Stephanie McKibben, and the exceptional guidance, patience, and knowledge from my editors David Grandouiller, Angela Ivey, and Whitney McGruder. They have given me a profound appreciation for writing and editing, for which I am deeply grateful.

For those reading this page, thank you for being here. I extend my heartfelt gratitude for your reading this book and trusting me to impart my newfound knowledge of this cutting-edge subject matter. My hope is that you learned something valuable and enjoyed the journey.

It's been nine months since I started this process, and as I turn in my final manuscript, I want to acknowledge that this book came to be with the help and support of many wonderful people.

Avi, my love, thank you for being the supportive and loving human being you are—for fully understanding the space and time I would need, stepping in at home, reading drafts—there aren't enough words to express my gratitude and love.

To my incredible Gen Z children, Billy and Max, thank you for not balking at your Gen X mom writing about gaming but, in fact, educating me and warmly welcoming me into your worlds of *Fortnite* and *Minecraft*. Your love, encouragement, and remarkable patience have meant everything to me.

Thank you, Erica and Sasha, for your constant support and understanding.

To my brother, Carlos, thank you for your encouragement and always keeping me on the cutting edge of tech.

Lynn Casey, my writing buddy on the West Coast, who spent countless Sunday afternoons with me over Zoom, which I looked forward to every week. Our honest and energizing conversations and your inspirational words set my mind in the right place before we muted for our productive multi-hour sessions.

I want to thank the accomplished experts from whom I learned so much and who gave me their time and offered their expertise, insights, knowledge, and a big dose of passion and transparency: Kelly Cage, Lior Cole, Alice Delahunt, John Duffield, Hazel Evans, Adriana Hoppenbrouwer-Pereira, Kadine James, Natalia Modenova, Olivier Moingeon, David Ryan Mullins, Janey Park, Anne-Christine

Polet, Ivan Puzyrev, Christopher Screnci, Daria Shapovalova, Alex Smaga, Nancy Steidl, Sara Texeira, and Joaquin Tusquets.

Numerous people helped me cross the finish line, whom I want to sincerely thank.

Ben Tanzer, an accomplished author who, after reading parts of my draft, challenged me to tell the story behind the story. I would have never known to do that, and it made all the difference.

Paula Azevedo, a dear friend and amazing beta reader, suggested intelligent edits and asked the right questions, which helped me make it better. But mostly, she passionately encouraged me when the doubt set in. For that, I will always be grateful.

Ellie Preta, the super supportive sister-in-law who not only offered tremendous feedback and amazing support but also recruited her sister Cheryl Kitt, who added so much value that truly made a difference.

Felicia Walker, the honest, reliable, dear friend for whom I'm beyond grateful to always have in my corner and whose thoughtful feedback was the first to arrive, layered with love, encouragement, and exclamation points.

I'm beyond grateful for all the other friends, former colleagues, and new friends in the industry who lent their time and patience to be beta readers and give invaluable feedback: Jennifer Allain, Kathlin Argiro, Bobbi Beinhacker, Tom Boyle, Hazel Evans, Jody Heilbronner, Yelena Mogeletsky, Lincoln Moore, Michele Morcey, Catherine Nelson, MJ Quan, and Nancie Samet.

I'm humbled and grateful for all the early supporters; it has meant the world to me: Delta Alves, Kathlin Argiro, Paula Azevedo, Michelle Beinhacker, Nancy Carrell, Holly Cole, Laura Coleman, Mark Dos

Santos, Joan Dufresne, MaryAnn Dzinski, Courtney Elias, Hazel Evans, Cary Fappiano, Sofia Fernandes, Kathleen Lewis, Aliza Licht, Aditya Mani, Christine Marque, Bevin McArthur, Lincoln Moore, Jackie Moran, Alison Morano, Michele Morcey, Catherine Mouttet, Adrienne Niederreither, Masa Ostojic, Sheila O'Sullivan, Lara Pamoukian, Jennifer Paul, Ellie Preta, J. Carlos Preta, John Preta, Maria Preta, Maria Prince, Joyce Restituto-Carlin, Nancie Samet, Felicia Walker, Ashley Wick, and Dale Zeide.

Last but certainly not least, I want to thank my parents, who with their unyielding Portuguese-immigrant work ethic, their passion for design and craft—from clothing to stone walls—and their pioneering spirit, have been a constant inspiration in my life.

TO LEARN MORE ABOUT MY WORK:

Follow or connect with me on LinkedIn
www.linkedin.com/in/sonia-preta

Visit SRP-Consulting.com.

APPENDIX

INTRODUCTION

Bianchi, Tiago. 2023. "Global Mobile Traffic 2022." Statista. April 27, 2023. www.statista.com/statistics/277125/share-of-website-traffic-coming-from-mobile-devices/.

BigCommerce. 2021. "2021 Consumer Spending Trends: An Omnichannel Report." *BigCommerce* (blog). Accessed June 8, 2023. grow.bigcommerce.com/rs/695-JJT-333/images/2021_consumer_spending_trends_paypal_zettle_en_us.pdf.

Big Think. 2022. "The Metaverse Explained in 14 Minutes | Matthew Ball." *Big Think* (blog). August 26, 2022. 14:38. youtu.be/4S-4mTvK4cI.

Lebow, Sara. 2022. "The Future of Social Commerce from Facebook to Instagram to TikTok." *Insider Intelligence* (blog). November 14, 2022. www.insiderintelligence.com/content/future-of-social-commerce-facebook-instagram-tiktok.

McKinsey & Company. 2022. "Value Creation in the Metaverse." *McKinsey & Company* (blog). June 14, 2022. www.mckinsey.com/capabilities/growth-marketing-and-sales/our-insights/value-creation-in-the-metaverse.

Mohsin, Maryam. 2022. "10 Online Shopping Statistics You Need to Know in 2023 [Infographic]." *Oberlo* (blog). November 13, 2022. www.oberlo.com/blog/online-shopping-statistics.

CHAPTER 1: DISCOVERING THE METAVERSE

Ball, Matthew. 2022. *The Metaverse: And How It Will Revolutionize Everything*. New York, NY: Liveright.

Boulevard Staff. 2022. "Lessons from the Best in Tech: Epic Games & Fortnite." *Boulevard* (blog). August 30, 2022. www.joinblvd.com/blog/lessons-from-the-best-in-tech-fortnite/.

Hu, Krystal. 2023. "CHATGPT Sets Record for Fastest-Growing User Base—Analyst Note." *Reuters* (blog). February 2, 2023. www.reuters.com/technology/chatgpt-sets-record-fastest-growing-user-base-analyst-note-2023-02-01/.

Iqbal, Mansoor. 2023. "Fortnite Usage and Revenue Statistics (2023)." *Business of Apps* (blog). January 9, 2023. www.businessofapps.com/data/fortnite-statistics/.

NVIDIA. 2023. "Nvidia and Microsoft to Bring the Industrial Metaverse and AI to Hundreds of Millions of Enterprise Users via Azure Cloud." June 8, 2023. nvidianews.nvidia.com/news/nvidia-and-microsoft-to-bring-the-industrial-metaverse-and-ai-to-hundreds-of-millions-of-enterprise-users-via-azure-cloud.

Rojas, Juanma. 2022. "NFTs and Their Relationship with the Blockchain." *Telefónica* (blog). September 5, 2022. www.telefonica.com/en/communication-room/blog/nfts-and-their-relationship-with-the-blockchain/.

Stevenson, Seth. 2020. "The Road to *Fortnite*." *Slate* (blog). June 16, 2020. slate.com/business/2020/06/fortnite-success-epic-games-tim-sweeney.html.

Takahashi, Dean. 2022. "Bain Predicts Gaming Will Grow 50% to $300 Billion in 5 Years." *VentureBeat* (blog). October 13, 2022. venturebeat.com/games/bain-predicts-gaming-will-grow-50-to-300-billion-in-5-years/.

Velasquez, Fran. 2023. "AI Will 'Accelerate' the Metaverse, Empower Creators: The Sandbox Co-Founder." *CoinDesk* (blog). April 13, 2023. www.coindesk.com/web3/2023/04/13/ai-will-accelerate-the-metaverse-empower-creators-the-sandbox-co-founder/.

CHAPTER 2: ONLINE SHOPPING—WHAT HAS BEEN MISSING?

Chan, Stephanie. 2021. "TikTok Becomes the First Non-Facebook Mobile App to Reach 3 Billion Downloads Globally." *Sensor Tower Inc* (blog). July 2021. sensortower.com/blog/tiktok-downloads-3-billion.

Gagliese, Joe. 2022. "Council Post: The Rise of the Influencer: Predictions for Ways They'll Change the World." *Forbes* (blog). July 11, 2022. www.forbes.com/sites/theyec/2022/07/08/the-rise-of-the-influencer-predictions-for-ways-theyll-change-the-world/.

Gentry, Amy. 2023. "Inside Carla Rockmore's Famous and Fabulous Dallas Closet." *Texas Monthly*, January 2023. www.texasmonthly.com/style/carla-rockmore-closet-dallas-tiktok/.

Ghaffary, Shirin, and Alex Heath. 2022. "The Facebookification of Instagram." *Vox* (blog). July 27, 2022. www.vox.com/recode/23274761/facebook-instagram-land-the-giants-mark-zuckerberg-kevin-systrom-ashley-yuki.

History Computer Staff. 2022. "Instagram: Complete Guide—History, Products, Founding, and More." *History Computer* (blog). November 30, 2022.
history-computer.com/instagram-history/.

Jain, Nimisha. 2021. "The Joy of Shopping—And How to Recapture It Online." Filmed January 2021. TED@BCG video, 11:14. www.ted.com/talks/nimisha_jain_the_joy_of_shopping_and_how_to_recapture_it_online.

Leiner, Barry, Vinton G. Cerf, David D. Clark, Robert E. Kahn, Leonard Kleinrock, Daniel C. Lynch, Jon Postel, Larry G. Roberts, and Stephen Wolff. 2022. "Brief History of the Internet." *Internet Society* (blog). September 22, 2022.
www.internetsociety.org/internet/history-internet/brief-history-internet/.

Lewis, Jordan Gaines. 2012. "Clothes Make the Man-Literally." *Psychology Today* (blog). August 24, 2012.
www.psychologytoday.com/us/blog/brain-babble/201208/clothes-make-the-man-literally.

Moran, Kate. 2022. "Why So Many Luxury Brands Are Terrible at Ecommerce." *Nielsen Norman Group* (blog). May 29, 2022.
www.nngroup.com/articles/luxury-terrible-ecommerce/.

Paul, Kari. 2023. "Thousands of Meta Workers Hit by New Round of Layoffs as Company Cuts Costs." *The Guardian*, April 19, 2023.
www.theguardian.com/technology/2023/apr/19/meta-layoffs-facebook-cuts-workers.

Ruby, Daniel. 2023. "71+ Instagram Statistics for Marketers in 2023 (Data & Trends)." *DemandSage* (blog). April 7, 2023.
www.demandsage.com/instagram-statistics/.

The Economist. 2022. "How Will Businesses Use the Metaverse?" *The Economist* (blog). November 24, 2022. 21:09.
www.youtube.com/watch?v=LEgHRAQ1HmE.

Webley, Kayla. 2010. "A Brief History of Online Shopping." *Time*, July 2010.
content.time.com/time/business/article/0,8599,2004089,00.html.

Worldometer. n.d. "Current World Population." Worldometer. Accessed May 24, 2023.
www.worldometers.info/world-population/.

CHAPTER 3: SELF-EXPRESSION

Alo Yoga. 2022. "Alo Yoga Brings Wellness to the Metaverse with Roblox." *PR Newswire* (blog). February 10, 2022.
www.prnewswire.com/news-releases/alo-yoga-brings-wellness-to-the-metaverse-with-roblox-301479855.html.

Bari, Shahidha. 2020. *Dressed: A Philosophy of Clothes.* New York City, NY: Basic Books.

Barry, Samantha. 2022. "Vogue Business Editor Maghan McDowell & Alice Delahunt on The Metaverse, Digital Fashion, and Crypto (Oh My!)" *She Makes Money Moves | Glamour.* November 2, 2022. 47 min.
podcasts.apple.com/us/podcast/vogue-business-editor-maghan-mcdowell-alice-delahunt/id1474398837?i=1000584757572.

Brown, Mike. 2023. "The Finances of Fortnite: How Much Are People Spending on This Game?" *LendEDU* (blog). April 5, 2023.
lendedu.com/blog/finances-of-fortnite/.

Iqbal, Mansoor. 2023. "Fortnite Usage and Revenue Statistics (2023)." *Business of Apps* (blog). January 9, 2023.
www.businessofapps.com/data/fortnite-statistics/.

Voxburner Content Team. 2022. "Here's How Many Gen Zers Have Spent Money on Virtual Items within a Game." *Voxburner* (blog). September 1, 2022.
www.voxburner.com/blog/gen-z-gaming-spends/.

CHAPTER 4: GAMING AND VIRTUAL WORLDS

Academy of Interactive Arts & Sciences. 2022. "Realizing Our Full Potential to Lead the Modern Entertainment Industry | EA's Laura Miele #DICE2022." Academy of Interactive Arts & Sciences. May 17, 2022. 28:55.
www.youtube.com/watch?v=lsHcCAN1er0.

Ball, Matthew. 2022. *The Metaverse: And How It Will Revolutionize Everything*. New York, NY: Liveright.

Branka. 2023. "Generation Z Statistics 2023." *TrueList* (blog). January 7, 2023.
truelist.co/blog/generation-z-statistics/.

Campbell, Graeme. 2021. "Video Game Fashion Is Cool, Assuming You Can Afford It." *Highsnobiety* (blog). September 21, 2021.
www.highsnobiety.com/p/balenciaga-fortnite-video-game-fashion/.

D'Angelo, Enrico. 2023. "Our Vision for the Roblox Economy." Roblox Blog, July 18, 2023.
blog.roblox.com/2023/07/vision-roblox-economy/.

Eldad, Asaf. 2023. "Unity vs Unreal, Which Kind of Game Dev Are You?" *Incredibuild* (blog). January 30, 2023.
www.incredibuild.com/blog/unity-vs-unreal-what-kind-of-game-dev-are-you.

Ernest, Maya. 2021. "A Virtual Gucci Bag Sold for over $4,000—More than the Real Deal." *Input* (blog). May 25, 2021. www.inverse.com/input/style/roblox-gucci-bag-handbag-purse-digital-virtual-nft-sold-4000.

Gonzalez-Rodriguez, Angela. 2022. "Tried and Tested Revenue Streams for Fashion Brands in the Metaverse." *FashionUnited* (blog). October 17, 2022. fashionunited.uk/news/business/tried-and-tested-revenue-streams-for-fashion-brands-in-the-metaverse/2022101665708.

Hill, Simon. 2021. "What You Need to Know about Roblox—and Why Kids Are Obsessed." *Wired* (blog). March 15, 2021. www.wired.com/story/unpacking-roblox-and-its-popularity/.

Howarth, Josh. 2023. "How Many Gamers Are There? (New 2023 Statistics)." *Exploding Topics* (blog). January 18, 2023. explodingtopics.com/blog/number-of-gamers.

Jones, Rachyl. 2022. "House of Blueberry Has Been Outfitting Digital Avatars for a Decade." *Observer*, October 22, 2022. observer.com/2022/10/house-of-blueberry-has-been-outfitting-digital-avatars-for-a-decade/.

Kelly, Dylan. 2023. "LVMH Partners with Epic Games to Produce Immersive Digital Experiences with 3D Technology." *Hypebeast* (blog). June 14, 2023. hypebeast.com/2023/6/lvmh-epic-games-partnership-announcement.

Lee, Adriana. 2022. "Roblox Partners with Parsons on Metaverse Curriculum, Trend Report." *Yahoo!* (blog). November 1, 2022. www.yahoo.com/lifestyle/roblox-partners-parsons-metaverse-curriculum-153256523.html.

Maguire, Lucy. 2022. "The Digital Designers Making Millions from In-Game Fashion." *Vogue Business* (blog). May 25, 2022. www.voguebusiness.com/technology/the-digital-designers-making-millions-from-in-game-fashion.

McKinsey & Company. 2022. "Meet the Metaverse: Creating Real Value in a Virtual World." *McKinsey & Company* (blog). June 15, 2022. www.mckinsey.com/about-us/new-at-mckinsey-blog/meet-the-metaverse-creating-real-value-in-a-virtual-world.

Rousseau, Jeffrey. 2022. "ESA: 48% of Game Players Are Female and 29% Identify as People of Color." *GamesIndustry.biz* (blog). June 7, 2022. www.gamesindustry.biz/esa-48-percent-of-video-game-players-are-female-and-29-percent-identify-as-people-of-color.

Ruby, Daniel. 2023. "Fortnite Statistics for 2023 (Users, Revenue & Devices)." *DemandSage* (blog). February 7, 2023. www.demandsage.com/fortnite-statistics/.

Schafer, Josh. 2023. "Apple's Mixed Reality Headset Announcement Sends Unity Stock Soaring." *Yahoo! Finance* (blog). June 5, 2023. finance.yahoo.com/news/apples-mixed-reality-headset-announcement-sends-unity-stock-soaring-202949563.html.

Takahashi, Dean. 2023. "House of Blueberry Raises $6M for Digital Fashion in the Metaverse." *VentureBeat* (blog). January 16, 2023. venturebeat.com/games/house-of-blueberry-raises-6m-for-digital-fashion-in-the-metavese/.

Tassi, Paul. 2022. "Epic Reveals It Made $50 Million from One Set of 'Fortnite' Skins." *Forbes* (blog). November 9, 2022. www.forbes.com/sites/paultassi/2021/05/11/epic-reveals-it-made-50-million-from-one-set-of-fortnite-skins/?sh=5270a2363903.

Wootton, Christina. 2022. *2022 Metaverse Fashion Trends Report*. San Mateo: Roblox.

YPulse. 2023. "How Video Games Are Influencing Gen Z's Real Life Behavior." *YPulse* (blog). March 27, 2023. www.ypulse.com/article/2023/03/27/how-video-games-are-influencing-gen-zs-real-life-behavior/.

CHAPTER 5: EXTENDED REALITIES—XR, AR, MR, VR

Abualzolof, Peter. 2022. "Council Post: 5 Ways to Use Virtual Reality in Your Real Estate Business." *Forbes* (blog). October 12, 2022. www.forbes.com/sites/forbestechcouncil/2022/10/05/5-ways-to-use-virtual-reality-in-your-real-estate-business/?sh=341ef1057b1d.

Bain, Marc. 2022. "Will Brands Buy into a Virtual Version of Rodeo Drive?" *The Business of Fashion* (blog). March 28, 2022. www.businessoffashion.com/articles/technology/will-brands-buy-into-a-virtual-version-of-rodeo-drive/.

Ball, Matthew. 2022. *The Metaverse: And How It Will Revolutionize Everything*. New York, NY: Liveright.

Ball, Matthew. 2022. "The Metaverse Explained in 14 Minutes." *Big Think* (blog). August 25, 2022. bigthink.com/series/the-big-think-interview/why-the-metaverse-matters/.

Bilmes, Alex. 2022. "The Making of ABBA Voyage, According to the Mastermind Behind It." *Esquire*, July 22, 2022. www.esquire.com/uk/culture/a40665750/baillie-walsh-abba-voyage-interview/#.

Borrelli-Persson, Laird. 2022. "Everything You Need to Know about ABBA's Voyage Costumes." *Vogue* (blog). May 26, 2022. www.vogue.com/article/everything-you-need-to-know-about-abba-s-voyage-costumes.

Emperia. 2022 "Dior Beauty and Harrods—Virtual Experience." *Emperia* (blog). Accessed on January 13, 2022. emperiavr.com/project/dior-beauty/.

Empire, Kitty. 2022. "Abba Voyage Review—a Dazzling Retro-Futurist Extravaganza." *The Guardian*, June 4, 2022. www.theguardian.com/music/2022/jun/04/abba-voyage-review-a-dazzling-retro-futurist-extravaganza.

Huddleston, Tom, Jr. 2022. "Apple CEO Tim Cook Doesn't Like the Metaverse—He Predicts a Different Technology Will Shape the Future." *CNBC*, October 3, 2022. www.cnbc.com/2022/10/03/apple-ceo-tim-cook-doesnt-like-metaverse-prefers-augmented-reality.html.

Indovance. 2022. "Digital Twins Is Empowering Airports Gear up for the Challenges of the Future—HKIA & Schiphol." *Indovance Inc* (blog). July 26, 2022. www.indovance.com/knowledge-center/digital-twins-is-empowering-airports-gear-up-for-the-challenges-of-the-future-hkia-schiphol/.

Intravaia, Ludmilla. 2021. "Le Boudoir Numérique Follows Natalie Portman in the Virtual World of Miss Dior." *Le Boudoir Numérique* (blog). September 28, 2021. boudoirnumerique.com/magazine-en/le-boudoir-numrique-follows-natalie-portman-in-the-virtual-world-of-miss-dior-59484.

Maisey, Sarah. 2022. "Abba Dressed by Dolce & Gabbana and Manish Arora in New Digital Voyage Tour." *The National*, May 27, 2022. www.thenationalnews.com/lifestyle/luxury/2022/05/27/abba-dressed-by-dolce-gabbana-and-manish-arora-in-new-digital-voyage-tour/.

McDowell, Maghan. 2023. "At NYFW, Web3 Efforts Backslide as Designers Shift Focus." *Vogue Business* (blog). February 14, 2023. www.voguebusiness.com/technology/at-nyfw-web3-efforts-backslide-as-designers-shift-focus.

Meige, Albert, Michael Papadopoulos, Juan Abascal, Primavera De Filippi, and Samuel Babinet. 2022. "The Metaverse, Beyond Fantasy." *Arthur D. Little* (blog). September 2022. www.adlittle.com/en/insights/report/metaverse-beyond-fantasy.

Morris, Ben. 2022. "'It Was the Best Day of My Life!' Guardian Readers on Abba Voyage." *The Guardian*, June 9, 2022. www.theguardian.com/music/2022/jun/09/guardian-readers-on-abba-voyage.

Nygaard, Safiya. 2021. "I Wore Digital Clothes for a Week." Safiya Nygaard. September 24, 2021. 28:16. www.youtube.com/watch?v=qVfJheBp7Ys.

Nygaard, Safiya (@safiyany). 2021. "The Mitochondria May Be the Powerhouse of the Cell, but I Look like the Golgi Body." Instagram, September 1, 2021.

Snap Inc. 2023. "SPS 2023: Making Snapchat Your Most Personal Camera." *Snap Newsroom* (blog). April 19, 2023. newsroom.snap.com/sps-2023-making-snapchat-your-most-personal-camera.

CHAPTER 6: NFTS AND THE BLOCKCHAIN

Akhtar, Tanzeel, Emily Nicolle, and Anna Irrera. 2022. "Luxury Brands Gucci, Tiffany Dive into NFTs despite Slump." *Bloomberg* (blog). August 3, 2022. www.bloomberg.com/news/articles/2022-08-03/luxury-brands-gucci-tiffany-co-dive-into-nfts-despite-slump?leadSource=uverify+wall.

Canny, Will. 2023. "Metaverse Gaming, NFTs Could Account for 10% of Luxury Market by 2030: Morgan Stanley." *CoinDesk* (blog). May 11, 2023. www.coindesk.com/business/2021/11/22/metaverse-gaming-nfts-could-account-for-10-of-luxury-market-by-2030-morgan-stanley/.

Christie's (@Christie'sInc). 2021. "@beeple's 'The First 5000 Days', the 1st purely digital NFT based artwork offered by a major auction house has sold for $69,346,250, positioning him among the top three most valuable living artists. Major Thanks to @beeple + @makersplaceco. More details to be released shortly." Twitter, March 11, 2021, 8:04 am.

DeAcetis, Joseph. 2021. "How the NFT Boom and Luxury Fashion Brands Are Aiming for Success." Forbes (blog). September 20, 2021. www.forbes.com/sites/josephdeacetis/2021/09/20/how-the-nft-boom-and-luxury-fashion-brands-are-aiming-for-success/.

Dey, Victor. 2023. "How Blockchain Technology Is Paving the Way for a New Era of Cloud Computing." *VentureBeat* (blog). April 28, 2023. venturebeat.com/data-infrastructure/how-blockchain-technology-is-paving-the-way-for-a-new-era-of-cloud-computing/.

Hissong, Samantha. 2021. "How Four NFT Novices Created a Billion-Dollar Ecosystem of Cartoon Apes." *Rolling Stone* (blog). November 1, 2021. www.rollingstone.com/culture/culture-news/bayc-bored-ape-yacht-club-nft-interview-1250461/.

Mapperson, Joshua. 2021. "Beeple NFT Sells for Record $6.6M as Bidding for 'Everydays' at Christie's Hits $2.2M." *Cointelegraph* (blog). February 26, 2021. cointelegraph.com/news/beeple-nft-sells-for-record-6-6m-as-bidding-for-everydays-at-christie-s-hits-2-2m.

Ramaswamy, Anita, and Lucas Matney. 2022. "Athleisure Icon Ty Haney Raises $9.8M in Fresh Funding for Her Blockchain Rewards Startup." *TechCrunch* (blog). June 6, 2022. techcrunch.com/2022/06/02/outdoor-voices-athleisure-founder-ty-haney-blockchain-crypto-consumer-brands-startup-chain-reaction/.

Ryder, Bethanie. 2022. "Gucci Appointed a Head of Metaverse. Should Luxury Follow Suit?" Jing Daily (blog). October 24, 2022. jingdaily.com/gucci-head-of-metaverse/.

Schulz, Madeleine. 2023. "Alo Yoga Rolls Out Digital Twins to Accompany Its Premium Ski Collection." *Vogue Business* (blog). February 1, 2023. www.voguebusiness.com/technology/alo-yoga-rolls-out-digital-twins-to-accompany-its-premium-ski-collection.

Sinclair, Isabelle. 2023. "NFTs and Luxury Fashion: A Conscious Coupling." *L'OFFICIEL USA* (blog). February 14, 2023. www.lofficielusa.com/fashion/nfts-luxury-fashion-collaborations-gucci-louis-vuitton.

SXSW. 2022. "BEEPLE & Laurie Segall | SXSW 2022," *SXSW* (blog). May 16, 2022. 1:03:39. www.youtube.com/watch?v=8EuL36HkhHM.

CHAPTER 7: BENEFITS FOR CONSUMERS

Adams, Robert N. 2020. "Minecraft X Uniqlo T-Shirts Coming to the Game (and Real Life)." *GameRevolution* (blog). March 2, 2020. www.gamerevolution.com/news/636335-minecraft-x-uniqlo-t-shirts-real-life-in-game-skins.

Anyanwu, Obi. 2021. "Moncler Enters Fortnite with Alyx Collaboration Collection." *WWD* (blog). November 19, 2021. wwd.com/fashion-news/fashion-scoops/moncler-fortnite-alyx-collaboration-collection-1235000841/.

Bein, Kat. 2023. "6 Luxury Brands with Explorable Space in Roblox." *Gotham* (blog). June 16, 2023. gothammag.com/ralph-lauren-gucci-nike-tommy-hilfiger-givenchy-roblox.

Clement, J. 2022. "US Video Gamers Who Made Social Connections via Gaming 2022." Statista. October 19, 2022. www.statista.com/statistics/1340350/us-video-gaming-community-social-connections/.

Debter, Lauren. 2022. "Fashion and the Metaverse: Why Ralph Lauren Wants to Sell You Digital Clothing." *Forbes* (blog). January 4, 2022. www.forbes.com/sites/laurendebter/2021/12/25/fashion-and-the-metaverse-why-ralph-lauren-wants-to-sell-you-digital-clothing/.

DELL. 2021. "Digital Clothing Is the Future of Fashion | Dell Talks with Daria Shapovalova." *DELL* (blog). August 11, 2021. 8:12. www.youtube.com/watch?v=iKBePuTOB6U.

Donald, Rachel. 2022. "Why 'Eco-Conscious' Fashion Brands Can Continue to Increase Emissions." *The Guardian*, April 9, 2022. www.theguardian.com/environment/2022/apr/09/why-eco-conscious-fashion-brands-can-continue-to-increase-emissions.

Edelson, Sharon. 2023. "H&M Launches Loooptopia, an Immersive Roblox Experience Where Fans Discover Their Digital Fashion Identities." *Forbes* (blog). January 5, 2023. www.forbes.com/sites/sharonedelson/2023/01/04/hm-launches-loooptopia-an-immersive-roblox-experience-where-fans-discover-their-digital-fashion-identities/?sh=6d55cb6b1013.

Entertainment Software Association. 2022. "2022 Essential Facts about the Video Game Industry." *Entertainment Software Association* (blog). June 10, 2022. www.theesa.com/resource/2022-essential-facts-about-the-video-game-industry/.

Faber, Tom. 2022. "Finding Community, and Freedom, on the Virtual Dance Floor." *The New York Times*, December 27, 2022. www.nytimes.com/2022/12/27/arts/music/vrchat-virtual-reality-clubbing.html.

Hooi, Ming. 2022. "Selfridges Launches First Metaverse Department Store in Decentraland." *The Mediaverse*, March 29, 2022. themediaverse.com/selfridges-launches-first-metaverse-department-store-in-decentraland/.

Jones, Luke. 2021. "Minecraft Gets x Uniqlo Skins Vol 2 to Dress Characters." *WinBuzzer* (blog). March 10, 2021. winbuzzer.com/2021/03/10/minecraft-gets-x-uniqlo-skins-vol-2-to-dress-characters-xcxwbn/.

Kelly, Dylan. 2023. "LVMH Partners with Epic Games to Produce Immersive Digital Experiences with 3D Technology." *Hypebeast* (blog). June 14, 2023. hypebeast.com/2023/6/lvmh-epic-games-partnership-announcement.

Kurutz, Steven. 2021. "Getting Married in the Metaverse." *The New York Times*, December 8, 2021. www.nytimes.com/2021/12/08/fashion/metaverse-virtual-wedding.html.

Lacoste. 2022. "Lacoste X Minecraft—It All Begins with Play." *Lacoste* (blog). March 14, 2022. corporate.lacoste.com/lacoste-x-minecraft-it-all-begins-with-play/.

Lloyd-Smith, Harriet. 2022. "Louis Vuitton Marks 200th Birthday with Art Video Game." *Wallpaper** (blog). October 7, 2022. www.wallpaper.com/art/louis-vuitton-video-game-200th-anniversary.

Mahlich, Hetty. 2022. "Chanel Makes Their First Metaverse Move for Virtual Reality Experience 'Le Bal de Paris.'" *SHOWstudio* (blog). May 25, 2022. showstudio.com/news/chanel-make-their-first-metaverse-move-for-virtual-reality-experience-le-bal-de-paris.

Newton, Casey. 2021. "Mark in the Metaverse." *The Verge* (blog). July 22, 2021. www.theverge.com/22588022/mark-zuckerberg-facebook-ceo-metaverse-interview.

Owusu, Beverlyn. 2022. "Fashion Brands That Have Partnered with Sandbox." *Your Own Creativity* (blog). May 9, 2022. www.theyoc.com/blog/fashion-brands-that-have-partnered-with-sandbox.

Schulz, Madeleine. 2022. "Burberry Partners with Minecraft as It Goes Deeper into Gaming." *Vogue Business* (blog). November 1, 2022. www.voguebusiness.com/technology/burberry-partners-with-minecraft-as-it-goes-deeper-into-gaming.

Smith, P. 2022. "Rental Apparel Revenue Worldwide 2026." Statista. January 28, 2022.

https://www.statista.com/statistics/1195613/rental-apparel-market-revenue-worldwide/.

Taub, Eric A. 2008. "It's Not a Game Console, It's a Community." *The New York Times*, July 21, 2008. archive.nytimes.com/bits.blogs.nytimes.com/2008/07/21/its-not-a-game-console-its-a-community/.

Vogels, Emily A., Risa Gelles-Watnick, and Navid Massarat. 2022. "Teens, Social Media and Technology 2022." *Pew Research Center* (blog). August 10, 2022. www.pewresearch.org/internet/2022/08/10/teens-social-media-and-technology-2022/.

Walk-Morris, Tatiana. 2022. "Bloomingdale's Debuts Virtual Department Store for the Holidays." *Retail Dive* (blog). November 21, 2022. www.retaildive.com/news/bloomingdales-emperia-virtual-department-store-holidays/637007/.

CHAPTER 8: A CREATOR'S PARADISE

Bonilla, Yarimar. 2023. "Bad Bunny Is [Winning in Non-English]." *The New York Times,* February 11, 2023. www.nytimes.com/2023/02/11/opinion/bad-bunny-non-english-grammys.html.

Hall, Christine. 2023. "Luxury Fashion Meets Blockchain on SYKY, the Seven Seven Six-Backed Web3 Platform." *TechCrunch* (blog). January 17, 2023. techcrunch.com/2023/01/17/luxury-fashion-syky-seven-seven-six-web3/.

Jennings, Rebecca. 2022. "So Your Kid Wants to Be an Influencer." *Vox* (blog). August 31, 2022. www.vox.com/the-goods/2022/8/31/23328677/kid-influencer-ryans-world-ellie-zeiler.

Matney, Lucas. 2022. "Avatar Startup Genies Hits 1 Billion Valuation in Latest Raise." *TechCrunch* (blog). April 12, 2022. techcrunch.com/2022/04/12/avatar-startup-genies-hits-1-billion-valuation-in-latest-raise/.

Morning Consult. n.d. "The Influencer Report: Engaging Gen Z and Millennials." *Morning Consult* (blog). Accessed May 30, 2023. morningconsult.com/wp-content/uploads/2019/11/The-Influencer-Report-Engaging-Gen-Z-and-Millennials-1.pdf.

Ramaswamy, Anita. 2022. "Star-Studded Digital Avatar Startup Genies Launches NFT Fashion Marketplace." *TechCrunch* (blog). August 30, 2022. techcrunch.com/2022/08/30/genies-celebrities-nft-fashion-marketplace-web3-warehouse-akash-nigam-influencers-creators/.

Samaha, Barry. 2020. "Balenciaga Launches a Video Game for Its Fall 2021 Collection." *Harper's BAZAAR* (blog). December 7, 2020. www.harpersbazaar.com/fashion/fashion-week/a34892239/baleciaga-video-game-fall-2021-collection/.

Semic, Sara. 2019. "Meet the Man behind the World's First Digital Supermodel." *ELLE* (blog). July 15, 2019. www.elle.com/uk/fashion/a28394357/man-behind-worlds-first-digital-supermodel/.

CHAPTER 9: BENEFITS FOR BUSINESS

AN Editorial Staff. 2022. "Forever 21 Launches the World's First Metaverse-Tested Fashion Collection IRL." *Authentic Newsroom* (blog). November 30, 2022. authenticnewsroom.com/press-releases/forever-21-worlds-first-metaverse-tested-fashion-collection.

Business Wire. 2022. "Forever 21 Launches the World's First Metaverse-Tested Fashion Collection, IRL." *Business Wire* (blog). December 1, 2022. www.businesswire.com/news/home/20221201005082/en/Forever-21-Launches-the-World%E2%80%99s-First-Metaverse-Tested-Fashion-Collection-IRL.

Deloitte. 2022. "Try This on for Size: Metaverse Fashion May Be $55B Industry by 2030." *Deloitte* (blog). March 3, 2022. action.deloitte.com/insight/1514/try-this-on-for-size:-metaverse-fashion-may-be-dollar55b-industry-by-2030.

Dogadkina, Olga. 2022. "Why Retailers Are Racing to Have a Metaverse Presence." *Forbes* (blog). October 14, 2022. www.forbes.com/sites/forbestechcouncil/2022/10/14/why-retailers-are-racing-to-have-a-metaverse-presence/?sh=aceea34262a1.

Ginsburg, Randy. "Feeling RSTLSS—Charli Cohen's New Drop, Warner X DressX, and Hello Kitty Trademarks." LinkedIn, December 20, 2022. www.linkedin.com/pulse/feeling-rstlss-charli-cohens-new-drop-warner-x-dressx-ginsburg.

Klasa, Adrienne, and Cristina Criddle. 2023. "What Gucci and Others Learnt from the Metaverse." *Financial Times*, February 24, 2023. www.ft.com/content/d4c3d51f-4568-400e-8ca9-7706539d9cae.

McKinsey & Company. 2022. "Value Creation in the Metaverse." *McKinsey & Company* (blog). June 14, 2022. www.mckinsey.com/capabilities/growth-marketing-and-sales/our-insights/value-creation-in-the-metaverse.

Obsess. 2023. "Introducing: Branded Avatars, a First-Of-Its-Kind Custom Avatar Technology by Obsess." *Obsess* (blog). Accessed on June 26, 2023. obsessar.com/blog-branded-avatars/.

PwC. 2023. "Experience Is Everything: Here's How to Get it Right." *PwC* (blog). Accessed on June 26, 2023. www.pwc.com/us/en/services/consulting/library/consumer-intelligence-series/future-of-customer-experience.html.

CHAPTER 10: RISKS AND THE COST OF INACTION

David, Sunil. 2023. "Why is 6G Required to Realise the Metaverse Vision." *Future Tech Congress* (blog). Accessed on June 8, 2023. futuretechcongress.com/blog-details/why-is-6g-required-to-realise-the-metaverse-vision.

Drawing Capital. 2020. "5G: The Revolution Begins." *Drawing Capital Research* (blog). November 20, 2020. drawingcapital.substack.com/p/5g-the-revolution-begins.

Dublin Tech Blog. 2023. "What the Metaverse Means for Sustainability." *Dublin Tech Summit* (blog). March 20, 2023. dublintechsummit.tech/what-the-metaverse-means-for-sustainability/.

Hatami, Homayoun, Eric Hazan, Hamza Khan, and Kim Rants. 2023. "A CEO's Guide to the Metaverse." *McKinsey & Company* (blog). January 24, 2023. www.mckinsey.com/capabilities/growth-marketing-and-sales/our-insights/a-ceos-guide-to-the-metaverse.

Linganna, Girish. 2023. "Virtual Reality, Real Dangers: The Metaverse Poses Counterterrorism Challenges." *The National Interest* (blog). January 1, 2023. nationalinterest.org/blog/techland-when-great-power-competition-meets-digital-world/virtual-reality-real-dangers.

Ramirez, Vanessa Bates. 2021. "The Metaverse Will Need 1,000x More Computing Power, Says Intel." *Singularity Hub* (blog). December 17, 2021. singularityhub.com/2021/12/17/the-metaverse-will-need-1000x-more-computing-power-says-intel/.

Teale, Chris. 2022. "Nothing Concerns the Public More about the Metaverse than the Misuse of Their Personal Data." *Morning Consult Pro* (blog). April 11, 2022. pro.morningconsult.com/trend-setters/metaverse-public-concerns-survey.

VERSUS. n.d. "Apple iPod Classic vs Apple iPod Nano: What Is the Difference?" *VERSUS* (blog). Accessed July 6, 2023. versus.com/en/apple-ipod-classic-vs-apple-ipod-nano.

World Economic Forum. 2023. *Guidelines for Improving Blockchain's Environmental, Social, and Economic Impact.* Cologny, Geneva: World Economic Forum.

Zdrzałek, Mateusz, and Cezary Michalak. 2021. "Web 3D Programming: Past, Present and Future." *Emphie* (blog). October 10, 2021. emphie.com/insights/web-3d-programming.

CHAPTER 11: WHERE TO START

Balis, Janet. 2022. "How Brands Can Enter the Metaverse." *Harvard Business Review* (blog). January 3, 2022. hbr.org/2022/01/how-brands-can-enter-the-metaverse.

Ball, Matthew. 2022. *The Metaverse: And How It Will Revolutionize Everything.* New York, NY: Liveright. E-book Format.

Deloitte. 2022. "Try This on for Size: Metaverse Fashion May Be $55B Industry by 2030." *Deloitte Development LLC.* (blog). March 3, 2022. action.deloitte.com/insight/1514/try-this-on-for-size:-metaverse-fashion-may-be-dollar55b-industry-by-2030.

Glover, George. 2022. "Goldman Sachs: These 4 Sectors Are Best-Placed to Benefit from the Rise of Web3 and the Metaverse, Which Could Represent an $8 Trillion Investment Opportunity." *Business Insider* (blog), January 18, 2022. www.businessinsider.com/metaverse-investing-goldman-sachs-web3-crypto-blockchain-analysis-outlook-strategy-2022-1.

Hecker, Melenie. 2022. "The Fabricant Is Giving You the Tools to Become a Digital Co-Creator." *The Stitch* (blog). June 24, 2022. www.wearethestitch.com/post/the-fabricant.

McDowell, Maghan. 2023. "AI's Revival Raises Questions for Fashion's Creative Class." *Vogue Business* (blog). January 10, 2023. www.voguebusiness.com/technology/ais-revival-raises-questions-for-fashions-creative-class.

McKinsey & Company. 2022. "Value Creation in the Metaverse." *McKinsey & Company* (blog). June 14, 2022. www.mckinsey.com/capabilities/growth-marketing-and-sales/our-insights/value-creation-in-the-metaverse.

Schulz, Madeleine. 2023. "Zero10 Wants to Crack Open 3D and AR Fashion Design for the Masses." *Vogue Business* (blog), February 8, 2023. www.voguebusiness.com/companies/zero10-wants-to-crack-open-3d-and-ar-fashion-design-for-the-masses.

CHAPTER 12: CONCLUSION

Bastian, Matthias. 2022. "Meta Halves Targeted User Base for Horizon Worlds." *MIXED Reality News*, October 16, 2022. mixed-news.com/en/meta-halves-targeted-user-base-for-horizon-worlds/.

Gaubys, Justas. 2023. "Apparel Industry Statistics (2014–2027) [Jan 2023 Update]." *Oberlo* (blog). January 2023. www.oberlo.com/statistics/apparel-industry-statistics.

Naysmith, Caleb. 2022. "Gaming Skins Just Became a $50 Billion Industry." *Yahoo! Finance* (blog). November 28, 2022. finance.yahoo.com/news/gaming-skins-just-became-50-143352555.html.

Roblox. 2022. "A Year on Roblox: 2021 in Data." *Roblox* (blog). January 26, 2022. blog.roblox.com/2022/01/year-roblox-2021-data/.